The Genius

E-Commerce

Mindset

By :
Belkeram Khaled

'The risk is your life, if you don't risk...'

Belkeram Khaled was born and grew up in the small Algerian town of Cheria, close to the Tunisian border. He attended USTHB in Algeria, a university that is located close to the capital city of Algiers, before he moved to Chicago, Illinois in 2012 and continued his studies at University Of Chicago.

He is an expert in the Internet and has subsequently gained qualifications in Digital marketing, Web Development and E-Commerce.

Today, Khaled is an online entrepreneur and manages his own online business. He still lives in Chicago, with his wife, and is passionate about all things to do with the Internet and helping others to make a success of their own online businesses.
When he has some free time and isn't working or writing, Khaled enjoys photography. He plays soccer at weekends and does voluntary work with several organizations both in Chicago and in his native North Africa.

Khaled's greatest wish is to see the whole world at peace and he believes that this possible with the internet helping to break down barriers and connect people from diverse backgrounds.
You can follow Belkeram Khaled and see what he is doing on his website at: www.KHALEDB.com

DEDICATION

Learning new things, especially the technology-driven stuff isn't always easy; the same applies in online business! But, where there are people with knowledge in the field and are willing to help, the journey to learning anything becomes much easy than one would imagine possible.

My voyage in the sea of online business couldn't have been smooth sailing without the help of many large heart experts and close people who made it fun and exciting for me.
To them, I dedicate this book!

I also need to thank you all, particularly the following people, for giving me the opportunity to make a success of my ecommerce adventure; I am most grateful for your help!

I want to thank all the digital marketers out there for making my experience in the dotcom-world a sweet feeling. Without your constant heads-up and desire to help, I may still be wandering in the lost island of click business, finding what works and what doesn't; but you saved the day, thanks again!

To my loving wife, exceptional dad, and mom in the whole world and indeed my entire family, you are the best! I couldn't have been where I am today, in the technology of doing business online, without your support, understanding and your continued help!

You guys are the ones who are giving me the reasons to forge ahead and make the most of the opportunity to make the world a better place through online business. Your being in my life is the tonic I needed to propel my inner strength to make things happen.

I will never forget my amiable teachers, coaches, gurus, and all my Facebook friends for your wonderful help. I have learned immeasurably from you all, and I believe the learning continues in the ever-changing world of ecommerce we have all made a home. I remain resolute in implementing everything I have learned from you for the good of humanity and I will continue to look up to your teachings in the coming days.

This book "Building a Successful Digital Business" was inspired by the need to give back and enrich the world that has given me so much; it is my humble contribution to extend the learning curve for people who want to know more about how online business works.

Without doubt in my mind, I know this will open your horizon to the enormity of great things every business and individual can benefit from ecommerce.

To everyone who made it possible, whom I may have left out in this dedication, you should know it was not deliberate, but I recognize you all. Your support for me to write a book on ecommerce is most appreciated; I am most grateful! Chokran .

Contents

Introduction

many books out-there they have too much content but nothing with more details , I had many book last year from amazon & most of them was only stories , motivations … witches good but many people was looking for more details , and more information like me to start my own E-commerce Business and scale it . That's why I come up with this book and I hop You Guys like it . I am not a professional writer but I can explain the e-commerce Game to you and give you most of the information that other people will never talk about it .This is will be the E-Commerce Golden Nuggets Overview That Will Help You To Grow Your E-commerce Business :

First ; Build Your Own Team :

    Owner (You)

    Team Member 1 : Project Manager

    Team Member 2 : Customer Service

    Team Member 3 : Product Specialist

    Team Member 4 : Supplier relations

Choose Your Own Team to be in House or Vertical assistance , It depence about the size of your business. & you Always can hire more or less . A team is incredibly important.

Know Your Business Term :

You have to know your business term:

-Are you short or long term?

-To Generate quick cash flow or build a brand to exit at a later date?

Both will determine your strategy.

Make Sure :

if the Shipping times too Long (in case if you doing DropShipping) , then Be prepared for angry customers, and a Lot of chargebacks/disputes if you are shipping from China and not transparent to the customer.

Always Make sure to make it clear to the customers and tell them How Long will take for the shipping before they place their order .

Have backup ad accounts for all the ads platform that you use the. Specially Facebook is on a rampage lately.

Keep on top of your P&L. Document each night your Profit and losses . Download and save copies off all invoices .

Use Google UTM Tags parameters for tracking , So You get the right Analytics , to make sure that You Scaling Your ads Right .

Use many ADS Platforms , don't stick with only one or two platforms . Don't Forget to setup your Retargeting ads right .

For The Facebook ads :

Set up how you read data

Frequency

Reach

CPM

CPC

CTR (Link)

View Content (FB Pixel)

Add to Cart (FB pixel)

Purchase (FB Pixel)

Cost per purchase

Purchase conversion value

ROAS

Amount spent today

Total amount spent

Common metrics on a winning products

1. Aim for less than $1.00 CPC

2. Aim for less than $10.00 CPM

3. Aim for less than $15.00 CPA

CPC = Cost Per Link Click

CPM = Cost Per Thousand Views

CPA = Cost Per Purchase

Test Stage (3 Days) :

PPE - $10 (Only used for social proof)

WC PUR - Testing 3 ad sets - one interest per ad set - $10 daily

Autobid - Newsfeed placement

Total Test Spend - $100

If no sales, move to next product.

Build Stage - (5 Days)

Take Your winning adset from above and duplicate to $20, $50, $100..If CPA is too much reduce

I prefer not to touch the budgets.

Feed the pixel. Cut the losers and duplicate the winners.

By now you are gonna see that one interest is going to perform better than the others. Maybe all three will.

Optimize the landing page or the product page:

Start working on AOV

Add Carthook, OCU or Design a Zipify page

Start creating your retargeting! DPA's

Install Recart

Start creating your first Lookalike audience of View Content. Build them all out! Then You can start testing it if you have enough data.

Order product to reshoot a better video.

Scale Stage - The Genius Ecommerce Mindset

14

The key is to find your winning formula (age, gender, placement, GEO etc) you gonna Use your ads platform metrics to find this , facebook or instagram or google ads.

Start the Scale into your ideal customer.and Duplicate the winning adsets again:

Duplicate to new campaigns and try IC, API, ADD to cart for facebook ads.

Scale to other countries.

USA - UK CA AUS NZ - and the Top 20 Countries .

Focus on LAA for cheapest CPA.

After that you should have enough data to scale hard to Lookalikes.(1% to 10%) try all of them sometimes 6% work better than 1% . (VC LAA, Add to Cart LAA, Purchase LAA, 75% of video, views LAA, 95% of video views LAA, Fan page Engagement LAA, Export Abandonment Cart, Emails LAA, Export Customer Emails LAA ...)

Instagram Influencers :

Do your research. A lot are overpriced! Focus on the accounts engagement. And real comments , and Have your VA contact accounts you like.

Send them the products and a t-shirt with the product logo and tell them to do a test post for 24H. Then you can start scale it with more influencers and sign a contract with them so they can promote your product for a period of time .

Affiliate marketing:

Have your own customers promote your products! Nothing it's more powerful than that. Offer them cash payment or an offers within your ecommerce website .

Email marketing :

Klaviyo or Mailchimp

Huge opportunity to increase profit ,After customer buys, send them a 24 hr one time offer with their confirmation. If someone subscribes but doesn't buy, send them a video introducing you and the company. Make sure you Segment the Email list , so you know exactly what & when you send your emails blasts .

Customer Service

You have to remember this "Customer is always right" . Outsource your customer service so you will have time to do other stuff and scale your business but stay on top of it, to make sure everything it's going right .

Golden Secrets :

- Apply for BBB accreditation. Trademark and LLC to protect your business .
- Read Books every day.
-Take breaks.

- Workout and do your meditation ..
- Success is a determinant of sacrifice and believe.
- Treat the customer like you would want to be treated.
- Understand your brand's target audience.
- Outline a mission statement for your website.
- Research great brands and learn from them.
- Add trust factors to your site.
- Figure out how to differentiate yourself from the competition.
- Set expectations from the get-go on every aspect of your business.
- Branding and logo are key. Pay extra for the branding design.
- Email weekly to convert non-purchasers on your list to purchasers and lifetime customers.
- Add blogging to your site and use customers to create content.
- Stay true to your goal. E-Commerce changes so quick, don't just abandon your vision because of latest trends and speculative chat. Test before you make big decisions.
- Treat fan pages as major assets.
- make sure you have a presence on all social media.
- Be innovative and daring.
- Sell unique products!
- Have 24-7 VA's.
- Scale your business Internationally once equipped to handle the volume.
- Win or learn (If you win, GREAT… If you don't, you learn!).

Chapter 1:

Everything it's about your Mindset

Henry Ford famously said: "Whether you think you can or think you can't – you're right."

This quote has been used endlessly and demonstrates the fact that your mindset directly impacts everything in business. Whether you've had a long day, woken up late, forgotten your lunch or received some bad news, the way you react to this will determine your success.

While a mindset can be negative, full of stress or frustration, similarly, it can be positive, used to push you towards your goals and objectives. It is your own decision whether you allow unexpected occurrences to negatively impact your mindset, or whether you work towards progress and stay focused.

A mindset was described as "a mental frame or lens that selectively organises and encodes information, thereby orienting an individual toward a unique way of understanding an experience and guiding one toward corresponding actions and responses" by the Stanford Mind and Body Lab. Your mindset has the power to affect judgement, motivation and much more.

Prestigious psychologist and author of Working Minds: A Practitioner's Guide to Cognitive Task Analysis, Gary Klein, explained that your mindset is more than just an attitude or temporary thought.

Klein highlights the fact that a mindset is an entire way of thinking, determining reactions, preferences and ways we tend to behave. Mindsets determine our focus, meaning we know what to aim towards, pay most attention to, and which information to digest. Mindsets give us guidance and a path of action, with Klein adding: "When our mindsets become habitual, they define who we are, and who we can become."

In addition to this, it has been proven that having a positive mindset elongates the average person's life by an incredible 7.5 years.

Stanford University's Dr. Carol Dweck who wrote the highly proclaimed Mindset: The New Psychology of Success, closely looked into the mindset of students in relation to their educational outcomes. She said: "For 20 years, my research has shown that the view you adopt for yourself profoundly affects the way you lead your life." Dr. Dweck's beliefs centred largely around the idea that students created a large portion of their own success through their mindsets, with those who believed in their abilities and who remained positive about potential outcomes applying themselves more to their studies than those who maintained a negative outlook. Those which believed in themselves and their ability to improve put in additional time and work to grow, ultimately resulting in greater achievements, which she called "the growth mindset." Those who remained negative about the possibilities were called "the fixed mindset" by Dr Dweck. Her main point was that attitudes enormously impact your achievements in life. Those who spend time concerned about negative aspects of life, or focusing on things which haven't gone to plan will find themselves increasingly stressed and upset. On the other hand, those who choose to pay particular attention to positives in the world will keep a happy, healthy and empowered mindset.

Changing Your Mindset

Mindsets are not set, in fact they can be changed, adapted and altered over time through the decision to change. While it doesn't happen overnight, these differences are noticeable and bring endless benefits.

Business owner Thomas Despin spoke about the importance of his team's mindset. He noted large negative impacts when the group mentality was low, for example when stressed or not confident, this was clear, impacting all members of the team even when it had only been one of two within the team originally. He called this a "poor mindset."

Contrastingly, what Despin described as a "rich mindset" was a great team mentality, encouraging each other, prioritising and working efficiently. This was proven to bring great success to the business in all areas, signifying the importance of your mindset, whether as an individual or as part of a team.

While I already touched on the power the brain has and how it can influence decisions automatically without you even being aware, this links with mindsets. Just as we prefer and stick to things we are most familiar with, we also do the same with ways of thinking. If we have been living with a negative mindset for a long period of time, focusing on the bad aspects of things and ignoring the positives, this can easily become automatic.

Our entire lives can be shaped by this mindset, with beliefs, aspirations, work ethic and dreams being influenced by what you believe is possible.

Think about the people you know. Without even having to think, you can probably name certain people who act defeated without even attempting something, and other people who remain positive and strong regardless of the situation. These people tend to follow the patterns they have set for themselves.

This mindset influences every business decision made, the impression you make in a business meeting and other people's outlook on your products. For this reason, it's vital to maintain a healthy mindset in order to succeed in business, turning entrepreneurs into market leaders.

Those who struggle to find a positive mindset often feel trapped, unable to fix or improve their way of thinking. However, a positive mindset can begin as quickly as a negative mindset did, making it possible for absolutely anybody, albeit with a little work.

The only way to turn a mindset around is to force change. You have to want it, retraining your brain towards unfamiliar thought processes, which does require a level of dedication and effort.

Here's how to retrain your mindset:

1. Understand your mindset – Do you think you have traits of a negative mindset? What concerns you? Do you struggle to become motivated? Do you prefer to sail through life as opposed to grafting for results? Are you scared of failure? You must look into exactly how you work, where your downfalls are and how you could change this. Asking another person for an honest opinion can be a fantastic method of understanding your mindset, perhaps in ways you choose to ignore in daily life. Only through this analysis of your own performance and life can you understand the best way to reach your full potential.

2. Fight your negative mindset – When you see patterns forming, or feel a negative trait shaping your thoughts or actions, you must choose to go against this. The next time you are presented with a challenge and find yourself thinking "there's no point in trying this", you must decide not to believe this. Instead, you must push yourself into the situation, giving 100% effort and instead telling yourself "I've learnt new things before, and can apply existing knowledge to this. Anything I don't know, I can learn with the help of others." Saying this out loud often helps to reinforce this new thought process in your mind, or you can even have a chat with colleagues or acquaintances about the new challenge. This is an effective way to not only re-shape

your own mindset, but motivate others around you in any business situation.

3. Act on your new mindset – Go for whatever you are telling yourself you can. Stop scrolling on social media, turn off the television and stop any distractions which may be hindering your progress. While it may seem unnatural and may not be particularly enjoyable at first, placing more importance on progress and changing your mindset to reach milestones or achievements will be worth the work. Sometimes, this new mindset can seem overwhelming. If this is the case, break projects down into smaller parts. Whether it's beginning with one paragraph of a 2000 word essay, or giving one client a call even when you have a list of 5,000. With small targets and areas of achievement, this will quickly become routine, gently easing you into your new mindset.

4. Don't be afraid to fail – Failure is an inevitable aspect of business. Every business owner will fail at some point, and it is up to you how you interpret this. Rather than letting failure dishearten you, you should use failure to grow, learn and shape future experiences. These times of failure are the most important to remind yourself that business in an ongoing project, not something which happens overnight. As such, you will be tempted to fall back into old mindsets but must resist temptation, assessing why and how you failed, what could have

been done differently, how you could have turned it back around and applying this to future experiences. This process continues to make you use your new mindset, turning failure into a valuable learning process which will enable you to succeed in business.

Qualities of a Mindset Wired for Success

In business, including e-commerce, you must harness specific thought processes, working alongside your mindset to contribute towards success. These steps can also help work towards a healthy and successful business mindset:

1. Positive mindset – Maintaining a positive mindset will help to stay free of negative thinking. Successful entrepreneurs are eager to learn, meaning even if they do not have a particular skill needed to succeed in one area, they will find a way to make it work. As such, people who have pessimistic outlooks on life are rarely part of any successful team, due to the impact they have on others and their levels of success. In business, you will also find many criticise. People are often threatened by success and sometimes those you hope would support you most choose to speak negatively about your work. This is often due to jealousy, as people are afraid to take the leap themselves, to begin their own business. You shouldn't waste your time worrying about these people's opinions, as they do

not matter to you. In addition, it is important to see hitches as hurdles and obstacles as opposed to the end of the road. Nothing is impossible to learn, overcome or outsource and the ability to keep your mindset positive and power through is what separates successful business owners from those that fail.

2. Focus on progress – Remaining focused on the overall goal as well as progress and small, continuous improvements stop you becoming stressed by details which do not need to be focused on. You must prioritise exactly what will enable you to reach these goals, not spending ages panicking about a slight design mistake, instead working on resolving, growing and continuing to push forwards. A successful businessperson will understand the most important aspects of business; acting as it's required, keeping employees' self esteem and team morale high and training effectively. They know what they want, where they're aiming to be in a year, and what the business plan is in 10 years. Before acting based on emotions or in the heat of the moment, a successful entrepreneur considers how their actions will benefit them in the long run.

3. Self pride – Any successful entrepreneur accepts who they are, their ambitions, goals and what they enjoy. They aren't afraid to analyse their own performance, highlighting the good and bad points within themselves. They know they aren't the best at

everything and accept help and new information to further themselves, even if it requires investment to ensure it is done to the highest standard

4. Realism – Realism will keep you grounded, remembering where you've come from, the path you've taken and how close you are to realising your goals. Mindsets aren't mind tricks to make you believe things which are not true and realism is vital in understanding your own business. Working within the e-commerce industry is a business which has benefitted many people, however it does not become a success for anybody without hard work and continuous building of your brand. You must successfully market to your target market, putting in countless hours of work to attract the attention of those you are looking to sell to. There is no shortcut to doing this and YOU have to give the consumers a reason to buy from you. Success doesn't come to you simply because of a good product. It's a combination of marketing, products, clever business decisions and dedication.

Remember: Nobody automatically cares about any brand. You must build this up over time through hard work, determination and a realistic view of what is required.

5. Remain focused – Your business must be your priority. If you take your eyes off the prize, you will become distracted and immediately not be able to grow your business as much as you potentially could. Money, time and effort should all be invested into making your project the greatest success it can be, never giving up and remaining dedicated at all times. A successful entrepreneur does not leave a project incomplete and continues to work harder and harder until all objectives have been met. If 100% effort is not given, you will not find success and all the time and money invested into your business venture will have been a waste.

6. Stay active – A successful businessperson does not wait around for the correct opportunity. They do not spend so long thinking about the dream scenario that they miss the opportune moment to launch. They will act and get the wheels in motion, regardless of whether or not they have completed the best marketing plan. They make do with what they have, building connections, working their way into meeting those they need to meet and looking to continuously improve. If you don't begin at some point, you never will as there is always room for further improvement and you would never launch if you waited for the project to be 'complete' beforehand.

Chapter 2 :
The Doing Mindset

There is a thin line between the conceptual and execution phase of a project, mapping out your plans on executing doesn't equal running the project. This has been a challenge for humans from time immemorial, finding that balance between idealizing and implementing. And it is one of the primary reason why most idea never makes it past the drawing board. When an idea comes crawling into your head, do you put in an effort to get it actualized or you get discouraged and they to dispose of its feasibility. Let's be pragmatic when you keep an idea at the conceptual stage, and you're putting so much weight on your shoulder than you can handle. There will be so much burden to bear, and you will end up changing your journal every month after getting it filled up with beautiful ideas. You try to exert a little effort, and they make it past 10% of the execution level and from there it becomes an unforgotten cause. In this world, there are two kinds of humans; the ones who put in efforts and gets required results and those who always ponder on ways to get results with zero attempts.

Your Actions Are A Representation Of Your Personality

Ensure you stay at the active side of life so that you won't be mentally redundant. As much as being hungry for good ideas is essential, so is being hungry for achieving results. The journey to achieving a result can be scary, I've been there, and I know why most people drawback from putting their thoughts into actions. A doer needs a right amount of grit, dedication and the resiliency all of this factor puts together can help you achieving success as an individual. Don't be fond of making excuses to shield yourself from executing the project. It gradually becomes part of you, and it becomes a trademark or something that defines you.

Let Your Action Be Your Talking Drum

There is indeed a great deal of success that comes from being an idealist, you plan and strategize, think of available resources and ways to put your plans into play. A well-planned intention that never got to execution stage is worse than a failed action. I have to be sincere, there is this inner satisfaction that comes with trying, but good intentions without actions brings enormous regrets. Let your actions speak for you, don't get complacent with being more of a planner and less of an executioners. You need the latter more than the formal. I employ you to take actions at every point in time, don't let the ember you've created in the planning stage gets quenched off even before seeing the light of day, due to your laxity orientation towards nailing a plan. Motivational books are good catalysts to spurn you into achieving but when you're stuck in the planning stage and probably convinced is the best course, a motivational book remains a lifeless object.

Holding On To The Thought Of Doing Is Exhaustive

The health repercussion of holding on to an idea without backing it up with actions is long time. You will have to shoulder the anxiety that comes with having a list of projects in your to-do list without the thought of making it happen. Your best bet is to thoroughly get rid of them or find a way to kick-start them. One thing that helped while I was deep in this same situation was to cut out procrastination, and once I have my mind made up, I set the ball rolling. Show concern for your wellbeing by working on your to-do list today.

Take That First Bold Step

What is lacking in most people is taking that first step which leads to the next, till it becomes iterative. Any idea that comes to your mind on a project don't waste your time get on it and see how far you can go. Remember the ability to get started helps you stay ahead. From that moment henceforth you begin to get the "first effect syndrome" which allows you to maintain a positive momentum towards becoming a doer. It is the momentum that will see you through other projects. It never stops it is continuous will work on you until you've been able to check your to-do list.

My motive behind this write-up is to snap you out of the thinking mode and embrace your reality. It doesn't have to be complicated or daunting, take it step by step. What matter most is getting it done not how much you did. I expect your heart to be burning with desires to get up and get going; the benefit is the gratification and the sense of accomplishment.

Chapter 3:

Customers don't think the way you do

One of the main lessons to learn in business is that you are not the customer. Because of this, you do not necessarily understand what they want.

To succeed in capturing the attention of your customers, you must create targeted copy, incentives, imagery and a sales experience which excited them. Only through doing this can you easily convert visitors into paying customers. It is so easy to forget that other people are the ones buying and tailor the experience to what you would want to see, how you would want to buy and the copy or imagery you would like to find. This is an enormous mistake. Customer research should always be done to determine your target market's preferences as opposed to your own.

Brooke Niemiec, the MCO of Elicit Consultancy said: "All too often, leaders think that their personal experiences with their brand are accurate reflections of all customers."

This is vital to remember, as while you may prefer bright colours and image-led websites, a potential customer may be deterred by this as they prefer neutral colours and text-heavy descriptions. For this reason, Brooke Niemiec's advice is vital. She added: "They make decisions based on what would personally make them happier and focus on details of the experience that matter to them. In doing so, however, they forget that many customers have different needs, interests, and experiences."

Following what you believe is exciting is an important part of any business, however taking others' opinions on board and acting on these is just as important, stopping you from spiralling off in the wrong direction when it comes to your business. You must look into the areas you don't want to hear, take criticism and sometimes even make changes to aspects of your business you were very fond of.

User experience is everything in business and plays an enormous role in creating loyal customers. While the majority of e-commerce customers buy on a mobile device, there are many who still prefer to use desktop versions of sites when making a purchase. It's important to make a user-friendly experience for those with all preferences, making it accessible on all devices, and finding a middle ground in many cases to keep the majority of potential customers happy. You cannot generalise your own opinion and assume it will be the same for your target market, even if you would personally purchase your products. You mustn't alienate your customers.

Using analytics to establish where your customers come from can be an incredibly useful tool, allowing you to design an experience from the user initially coming across the brand, to reading more messaging and eventually purchasing, making sure they enjoy every step of the way and are therefore inclined to purchase again in the future.

How to Get Out of Your Brain and Into Your Customers'

Often, business owners and entrepreneurs mistake their own preferences for that of the customer. In the process of doing this, they take what they would personally like to see and apply it to the situation, assuming somebody else would want the same.

For this reason, it is incredibly important to remember that you are not your customer and you may have differing taste when it comes to purchasing. By understanding this, you open the opportunity to further learn about this audience, perhaps undertaking consumer analysis and market research to perfect your business process. This can take incredibly long periods of time and can take place over years while a business strategy is already working. In addition, consumers' preferences always change, as do technological advances, social media platforms, website trends and competitors in similar industries, meaning there is continuously work to be done.

To begin to develop your business, you should create personas for each of your target markets. This could be a 30-year-old mother of three with no time, or an 18-year-old bodybuilder, depending on what you are trying to sell. Having these personas enables you to imagine what they may look for, as well as helping you to develop your understanding of this target market.

You should also question everything. If you find out that your target market spends an average of two hours in the gym every week, you must ask why. What would make them increase this time? Is this throughout the year or do they take time off at Christmas? Do they purchase more new equipment for the New Year to take on new challenges?

Finding the answers to these questions will help you to paint a more complete picture of your consumer. Perhaps you will find patterns in purchasing behaviour or work out the optimum times to post on social media to capture their attention. You may find that 70% of gym enthusiasts spend more on supplements than they do on personal equipment for working out, which could sway your choice in the products you offer.

There are endless benefits to understanding your target market, all of which can benefit your business and help to shape valuable decisions you may not have understood previously.

You should also speak to your existing customers and ask what they like about your business as well as what they feel could use improvement. Conduct market research on social media using polls or carrying out Q&A sessions. Not only will this help you to understand your target market, it will also show potential consumers that you care and are looking to improve.

Remember to use every opportunity to progress your business, using information to benefit the brand and further understand what makes the ultimate business and what your customers want. You may even find that this shapes decisions in the future as you gain answers you do not even know you will need yet.

This is the ultimate way to get out of your head, and into your customers'.

Create the Experience They Want

As I have already explained, we look to provide a service we would personally want to experience. We must remember that this is not only for us, but for the majority of customers, who may have differing requirements to ourselves. You must avoid falling into this trap which so many young businesses do, often causing them to ultimately fail. Keeping a regular to-do list and sticking to it is an effective way to not get side-tracked with your business' progress.

Use your research to create a checklist, for example, this could include; a neutral colour scheme on your website, daily social media posts, images of both males and females, introductory offers, photos of every product, online marketing and advertising, good customer service etc.

From here, you are able to ensure you meet each and every criteria your customers mention, putting them first and becoming more likely to win and retain their business.

Chapter 4:

Trust is the King

One of the first things to remember in business is that you are not a globally known brand. Simply and politely put… you are not Amazon. When a customer makes a purchase from a company they know, they know the exact process. They head to the website, search quickly for the item they require and make their purchase, possibly even having card details stored on the account. They are fully aware that their details are safe and usually know that buying on this site is an easy, painless experience.

But why do we trust the same sites every time? The answer is that we become familiar with them. We had a first positive experience, are aware that others use the site, most likely heard positive reviews and now know the process to make a quick and trustworthy purchase… what's not to love?

We believe the website will live up to expectations, and in most cases, in the likes of Amazon, the majority of products needed can be purchased on the website, with an ever-expanding range of products, items and services.

Your business cannot meet these expectations or cover such a vast range of products and you must also build a reputation before this automatic thought process occurs, which ironically can then grow your customer base rapidly in a snowball effect type of method.

Consumers do not naturally trust any site, brand or website. Until they have had a positive experience first hand and have begun to build a trusting relationship with your business, they will not trust you. This is a time-consuming process.

Eldar Sadikov, the Founder of Jetlore, spoke of the importance of customer retention, saying: "It costs five times as much to attract a new customer than to keep an existing one, so forging long-term relationships with customers is critical to any e-commerce retailer's bottom line and future company health." Highly experienced in retaining customers and supporting e-commerce businesses, Eldar's statement is incredibly valuable. The reason for this is that a happy, existing customer will return without the lengthy process required to convert a new customer. There should be regular benefits and reasons to make an existing customer stay, whether it's limited time offers, positive messages or even a Christmas card, reminding the customer that you care about their business.

Another hurdle you must overcome is the fact that customers opt to use well known sites before unheard of e-commerce companies. For example, some may go online to search for an identical product, on a reputable site they are familiar with, simply for peace of mind.

To combat this obstacle when starting out with new customers, it is vital to demonstrate your business as a trustworthy and reliable one. Reviews, videos, factual information and professional looking images are brilliant ways to grow the relationship between e-commerce sites and customers.

Making Sales = Signalling Trust

It is incredibly important to quickly capture the attention and trust of a potential customer, preventing them from going to competitors for their business. When money is involved, customers become incredibly wary of being scammed, strongly disliking the thought of parting with their hard-earned cash only to receive a sub-standard item, or even worse, no product at all.

It is a time-consuming process to build trust and a loyal customer base, with every single e-commerce site you see online going through the exact same process you will to get to where they are today. You can't expect it to happen overnight.

The main focus should be to remove any doubt the customer could have. Be transparent, clear and honest with your approach, offering customer service to put customers' minds at ease and build customer confidence. This is the best way to avoid sending customers to your competitors.

It's time to run through some of the factors which can reduce a customer's trust in a website.

Contact sections and customer service – You have to provide a decent level of customer service for a customer to trust you. They want to be able to contact you if there is a problem with an order, or if they would like to ask a question. Omitting a contact form is a huge warning sign for the majority of potential customers on e-commerce signs. After all, one of the major factors within e-commerce is customer satisfaction, the ability to return products and making customers feel they can trust you.

Have a secured website – Unsecured websites ring alarm bells for customers who would otherwise be willing to place an order. Entering your payment details is always a risk, and without some guarantee of the security of a website, it's been proven that an enormous 85% of those who shop online avoid unsecured websites. This doesn't have to be a time-consuming process, with SSL certificates being easily obtainable, greatly increasing the legitimacy of your e-commerce site.

Evidence of business connections – Consumers love to see reputable logos on a site, immediately filling them with confidence and assuring them that you are a legitimate brand which works with other well-known companies. This trust can greatly increase the likelihood of growing your customer base, whether through the simple appearance of a logo or a testimonial.

Clearly display company information – Prove that you are a real business with accurate company details and an 'About Us' section. Be proud of where your brand has come from, with images from your business and even 'Meet The Team' pages adding additional credibility to your brand.

Be clear with shipping details – It is beneficial to be transparent with operations. While you may sway towards not telling customers that their products are shipped from China and could take six weeks to arrive, this will result in unhappy customers and a loss of trust. To avoid complaints and to keep happy customers, be honest with the shipping process and provide as much information as you can, giving customers a full picture and helping them to trust you even more.

Demonstrate previous business – Customers of e-commerce stores rely heavily on reviews, whether they are curious about your legitimacy or even the quality of products. To build trust, you need honest reviews which are visible for potential customers. This will positively impact sales as it proves you have an existing customer base and also allows visitors to see what others thought of their experience with your brand.

Display terms and conditions – While we barely ever read full terms and conditions, there should always be a link available to these on a website, albeit small and not particularly prominent. Having these gives customers peace of mind and shows them you have nothing to hide.

Established payment gateways – Customers are incredibly wary of identity theft and often choose not to make a payment unless it is through a well known and reputable company such as Mastercard or PayPal. Ensure you have a reputable payment gateway to stop sales failing at the final hurdle.

Capitalize on Trust

To run a successful e-commerce store, you must capitalize on trust. While trust is one of the most time-consuming aspects of a business to build, it means new customers will buy from you, existing customers will continue to make purchases and potential customers will hear about you through loyal users of your site.

Once you have converted somebody to a trusting customer, you have done the hard work. As discussed earlier, it is far more difficult to convince an unfamiliar customer to buy from you. Once they like your service, they will opt to buy from you again before they choose one of your competitors.

With time, your reputation and brand awareness will grow, in the same way that Amazon's did, and eBay's did. Keeping a lifelong customer carries far more value than a one-time customer, meaning a beneficial, trusting and honest relationship is vital in order to become a successful business with regular orders.

Repeat customers and positive reviews will grow a brand without even putting any further work in, simply through providing a high-quality products and a positive experience. This should be combined with effective customer service and regular contact. Email marketing, social media campaigns and even courtesy calls can provide the opportunity to incentivise future purchases, keeping your brand at the forefront of consumers' minds and ensuring a loyal e-commerce customer base

41

who repeatedly purchase from you.

Chapter 5:

Don't Give a F*** About What Others Think About You!

Introduction

Today we've got a lot of people who are walking in the shadows of others, and they've never for a day embrace their reality. Every step they take in life is based on the "what he says, what she says", parents, siblings are driving force behind every decision they make. People like this can be regarded as being mentally lazy. They find it challenging to make vital decisions in life without the ones whom they love. This is no way nullifying the importance of seeking people's opinions to corroborate with your thought out plan but relying solely on them that it gets to the point of creating a psychological meltdown to your personality is dangerous. People with such attitude find its difficult to climb up the ladder of progress, in most cases, they experience the opposite. They gradually lose their grip and fall back down when there is no one to help them decide what they should be doing with their life. I have written this material for you on the best approach to stop caring about the disposition of towards you. Kindly follow me as I unravel necessary steps that help you to pay keen attention to your thoughts and yours only.

Take Opinions With A Full Understanding Of Its Rationale

The right approach towards considering the views of others is to analyze the premise or tenet behind it carefully. Is it because they genuinely care about you? Or you can sense an iota of selfishness in it? Take a wild guess of what might have prompted such advice. One example that readily comes to mind is when it comes to the issue of employment. Some children prefer to pursue their dreams of playing football or becoming a musician. Although your parents can see that you have the talents and vigor embedded within you, but they won't advise you on pursuing it. They would instead encourage you to find a means of sustenance that will help you to in becoming financially independent. No one is saying having a good source of income is terrible, but when it comes in the way of what you love doing, then it becomes more of temporary value. This is not a case of preaching against getting advice from your loved ones, far from it but evaluating the rationale behind such opinions.

To be pragmatic, nobody on the surface of the earth has a full measure of control on what you choose to do with your life, doesn't mean you should negate their opinions by when push comes to bun, it will be you against the world.

Regret Makes You Feel Unworthy

The example cited above is one of the too many reasons why people grow into depression and possibly which themselves death. They let the embers of their dreams and aspirations die off because they choose to listen. Have you visited a shelter for the elderly lately? Please do. You will get first-hand experiences of how they wanted their life to turn out and how it was shaped base on the opinion of others. There is no worst feeling compared to living with regret buried deep inside you. It will always eat you up like a terminal disease.

Feel Good About Yourself

When life throws lemons at you, don't just suck it up, find a way to make lemonade out of it. How far you will go in life depends on how much of a positive thinker you're. And this largely depends on how you let other people's perception affects you. There is a voice in your head telling you, how less you're worth and it keeps dampening your spirit. That voice is not you but the comments of others that you had to swallow from time immemorial. You might not be doing as much as you wanted in life, it's no reason to think you will never get there. It is not happening in your twenties doesn't mean it would never happen. Surround yourself with positive energy and continue to achieve greatness.

Surround Yourself With Positive Thinking Individuals

I always look out for the company of positive thinking individuals who see a bright future ahead, despite being bleak at the moment. Everything about them is strong right from their principle towards life and their relationship with others. You're beginning to know them, and you can feel the Cascade effect of their positivity boiling inside you. I have made friends with people who tried to make me feel unworthy and less needed. Would you like to know my protective mechanism? Spend less time with such people, if you find it difficult cutting them off. But if you can cut them off, then let them go with their negative inclination.

We've no doubt had a fantastic time going through this necessary steps of living our dreams and preventing the negative opinions of others from controlling us.

Chapter 6:
A School Doesn't Make An Entrepreneurs

Introduction

The recent uproar about matters concerning education has caused most people to question the true essence of going to school to learn fundamental knowledge about the real world. My point of view is not directed towards why people go to ask but to consider if book knowledge is needed in certain areas of life pursuit. Everyone needs education at least the basic ones that help to read, write and communicate with other people on a daily basis. I see no reason why someone that is inclined towards entrepreneurship will decide the best place to get cutting-edge entrepreneurial skills is from the four walls of a school. Going to school with the intent of becoming an entrepreneur is a total waste of time, money and every other resource incurred. This is no way saying going to college is bad, I mean I did go to college but spending time and money on things you can get free on the other side sounds like a waste of investment to me. Of course, some professions need the significant contribution of school knowledge and experience of teachers, but it's different with becoming a successful entrepreneur. I didn't write this piece to weigh my opinion on you, and it's more of seeing things from a different viewpoint. If every part of you signals entrepreneurship and you're making a move towards accomplishing it, then schools might be a wrong call.

Let me retract a little bit, the point I'm making is not to condemn going to school. Are you in school to become an engineer or medical practitioner? Then you need school. Are there less debt or no debt in your school fees or probably you're on a student loan? No problem. Do you want to move to a particular location and you know school will offer you that opportunity? Then go for it. But you're skilled in communicating with customers, and you can handle your sales and supplies without any lapses, then you don't need college.

The world has evolved, and there are so many things you can achieve without someone sitting you down to teach you, thanks to the contribution of technology and the internet. This milestone achievement must be recognized by student and parents likewise, that you can get yourself equipped about almost any knowledge you gain in school right in the comfort of your home at a fraction of the price.

Primarily what matters most in all of this, is to ignite my readers into action to help them achieve their dreams and not live a life filled with regret. And that's why I pen down most of my thoughts to send out messages that will move you to act not just read for relaxation or have a good laugh.

College education has being trivialized with the advent of the internet and technology. And with time when the internet makes learning more accessible it becomes more mainstream. For now what we're running in the system are more of brands such as Harvard, MIT, and so on. The accessibility tools will help us see those loopholes that colleges have been managed for long. Not all enterprise is capital intensive, and you can start a business from grand zero and find your way up the ladder. But college tuition fees says different you will be plunged into debt because you want to study about entrepreneurship. It means you become a debtor even before you start making earnings.

It is vital that you know what you want and clings to it. Don't be dissuaded by what others have planned out for you, not your parent or your peers own your future, let your conviction be your mouthpiece, speaking to your heart on what is right for you.

Conclusively, reading through this piece you will notice I have stretched out two vital points. That parents push their kids into debt through college loans to become a cut-edge entrepreneurial. Even if it comes with the purest of motive, it still doesn't feel right. And student wasting a critical period in their lives learning how to become an entrepreneur within the four walls of colleges. The issue here is not about going to college but spending an enormous amount of money to get a piece of knowledge that you can quickly get for free or at a tad bits cost. You don't have to break a bank to become an entrepreneur. That's the truth I'm preaching. If the inception of starting a trade puts you in a reoccurring debt, then you're in the wrong place.

Chapter 7:
Are You Under 30's ?

Introduction

Anxiety builds up when you're in your late 20s. It becomes increasingly daunting when you take a survey of your surrounding and see how well your age group are doing, and you begin to wonder why things are different for you. A got married, B just moved to his new house, C works in a multinational company, and so many things they made us believe makes you happy. Even when you choose to be indifferent people still draw your attention to these things at the slightest of opportunity. Then you begin to do a complete overhauling of your life, to see areas where you're not hitting the marks. What most people don't understand is that even at 30 you're just starting a whole new chapter in your life. You should never in a rush, see life challenges as a tunnel vision that will come in play in due time not when your parent says or your peer's opinion. You need to be aware of the expansivity you have in ages which implies that you can still live over 80 years which is five more decades. Pursuing dreams and struggling to make money is a treadmill that keeps iterating and it's best when you don't subject yourself to undue pressure. The best approach towards handling life pursuit is to take things one step at a time. Create a mental picture of yourself playing soccer, at this period in your life, is like reciting the national anthem, you're not even halfway into the match.

50

That is how being in your 30s looks like. I will share with you some vital steps that can help you maintain your focus regardless of your age.

Be Different And Outstanding

Working with other people's time will force you to work in the shadow of others and on the long run make you grow apprehensive. The frivolous things of life do not freak me since I'm entirely convinced that it's not a remedy for success. To some people, I appear a bit more as a mystery due to my decision and demeanor towards life. That man who is pushing himself way more than his tether in a bid to provide for his household is my mentor. I believe in the saying "not all heroes wear capes". Let's make a quick compare of two amazing individuals who have impacted in the game of basketball; LeBron James and Michael Jordan. When it comes to numbers of NBA title LeBron has two while MJ owns 6. That's enough makes MJ great. But when it comes to extending hands of kindness and showing concern for social justice, then Lebron wins it all. Although history might hold MJ a record holder of 6 NBA, people will never forget the good deeds of Lebron, and it will forever be crested on their heart.

Never Sell Yourself Short, Aim Higher

Have anyone told you lately that you're made of more? This implies that looking beyond within and thinking of dreams that takes a while but quite beneficial to your future. Immediate goals like making six figures are short term because it makes you limit yourself. So, after making money what happens next, probably make more money. And you might have to sell yourself short by involving in criminal activities to make your money. Think of goals like owning a private jet that takes you and your family on vacation and you for business trips. Every time you try to walk your way towards achieving your dreams, you're making a mark that will never go unnoticed in the history book.

Sever All Ties With Negative Minded People

If you're in your late 20s, you might find it hard moving on from people who are riled with negative energy, especially when you both go way back. It might even be a close relative like your parents. But keeping your sanity in check should be prioritized. If you're a positive thinker, it's healthy for you to find someone of like minds that will pummel you to achieve your dreams and even help you aim higher or encourage you when you feel certain things are unattainable.

For some who feel it's a good thing to do still finds it difficult to do. When climbing a ladder and you have people weighing you down with their baggage, you begin to struggle at every point to climb without falling. But imagine the amount of relief you will get the moment you drop that bag and how you can increase your pace and climb the ladder faster. That is an illustration of how you can be affected by people with negative energy.

Don't get discouraged or grow weary when it's not happening in your late 20s, never stop dreaming and you will attain your goals in due seasons.

Chapter 8:

How To Start a Mastermind

Introduction

Forming a mastermind always yield a positive result in your career growth. Finding people who have an equal or higher driving force towards achieving their goals is a plus to your professional journey. What makes the mastermind the proper dose for future development? A look at the definition will highlight point on why forming a mastermind group will contribute significantly to your growth. A mastermind is a group that comprises of people who are in the same position as you're in your life and they possess the spirit of a goal getter and striving collectively towards achieving them. Coming together as a group is primarily for self-growth, personal development, and self-gratification. It is more of working together to see areas where can develop ourselves individually. Iron sharpens iron, so they say, and we get upliftment by helping others grow. These are guiding principles of life which led to the inception of masterminds. You need to pay close attention to the number of group members which ideally should stand between four - five. Any mistake of going lower will bring about recycled ideas and cliché outcomes. The downside of going higher is the complete loss of the oneness and friendship that comes with joining a mastermind group.

Meetings should be on a regular preferably on a weekly basis, each member of the group speak out their fairs and success for that week, other members consider vital lesson as they can get from such wonderful experience. If peradventure they have something they've some problem that is impeding their progress the group can offer that member assistance.

A mastermind places your career on a pedestal when you ensure it is playing an active role in your profession. Each member of the group is expected to remain loyal to the group and ensure we collectively work together for a milestone achievement. Being a member of masterminds, you will be pummeled into going further in achieving goals. It holds you against your word and ensures you show resiliency, tenacity, and determination towards getting things done for yourself. It supports you in your high and low moments; this is what a healthy and forward thinking relationship requires. And you will get nothing short of that from a mastermind.

The Advantages Of A Mastermind

Support:

Your mastermind stays with you throughout the stages of your career, ensuring that you're at your best every time. They provide you with the huge backing towards achieving your goals, which is primarily why it was set up in the first instance. The good thing about mastermind is that we've varying experience on specific issues without result. It will be much more comfortable when other members of the group come with

54

suggestions which will guide in finding solutions to that problem. There is the peace of mind that comes with the fact that you have other people right behind you providing you with assistance every point when you need one.

Constructive Criticism

The fundamental cause for setting up the group is to provide insights through feedbacks. How much effort are you exerting? Is there any other way you can get things done? Are you in the right place in your career? Your group members will ensure you get insightful comments on how well you're faring. This is achieved through a round-table evaluation where down to heart suggestions that could immensely contribute to your professional development.

Accountability

There are so many hurdles that could drive us away from the part of success and avoiding them might not easy, since they surround us. Distractions are one of the too many hurdles, and other life pursuit can also drive you away from what you should be doing or what is needed to be done. Everyone sets goals, but the most difficult is keeping those goals in check and ensuring you're not drifting off that path. It will be a lazy approach when you do the keeping yourself in check by yourself without the contribution of an external body. It is imperative that you allow a third-party to point out where you can make needed changes. A mastermind offers you check-ins, follow-up, guidelines and they measure your progress and productivity level during meeting periods.

Insight

One the most amazing thing being among a mastermind is the understanding of who you're and where you're going. This grounded knowledge of each other assures you that you're giving your actual opinion which is based on your previous experience, not sentiment. You can only access yourself physically after dressing up through the mirror, just the people who see you physically can be the judge of how well dressed you. This same logic still applies you can get the real sense of how well you're doing in your profession if you don't permit me the evaluation of others.

Energy

The type of relationship they share in a mastermind is symbiotic. And this is one of the contributing factors that help each member in achieving greatness in their career. The positive energy among group members who are like-minded is contagious. This is why a mastermind is about going forward to bring your goals into a full circle.

Reality Check: my mastermind group has been instrumental in my journey through development at the start of my career till this moment. Being among this wonderful group of intellect has helped learn not to get comfortable with my way of doing things. All of these didn't come with a parting at my back, they critique my work and channel my energy in the right direction. I had a better approach to relating to clients, employers. They pointed out my weakness which is being too clingy to myself and not opened to suggestions.

What qualities define a strong mastermind?

Members Must Be Goal-Oriented

As individuals we all have goals and aspirations, they only come in varying types and magnitude. For a group such as this type, it is essential to share some basis in goal types. Take, for instance, I'm learning to start an auditing firm, and someone else wants to learn how to do breaststroke, you will see that there is a weird connection in that. But I'm starting my auditing firm, and another person is working on getting their already established company certified, that's a connection. It is not about specifics in most cases but the weight of your goals. If it's deserving of a mastermind.

Members Shouldn't Be Lukewarm

You must have something worthy to bring to the table and eat out of the table. Any member who is neither gaining nor contributing should be demanded to excuse the group since it's demeaning the real purpose of the group. You must have a goal, and everyone must be able to gain from you and vice versa. It is a symbiotic relationship, not a parasitic one.

Members Must Show Commitment

Commitment is essential to the growth of a mastermind. Each member must imbibe the culture of being present at meetings and also punctual.

You might not take note, but your attitude might have a cascade effect on other members of the group. Be tenacious and zealous towards fighting for the common good of every member of your team. Other members should also learn to be realistic with their demands, and they should not unnecessarily weigh others down with constant demands.

Members Must Have A Mutual Connection

If this is out of the equation, it becomes increasingly difficult for the member to share a good relationship and a oneness spirit. A good connection will grow into a strong bond that will bring out the essence of starting a mastermind.

The Process Of Mastermind

The fundamental elements of a mastermind are the availability and regularity for meetings. It is only when sessions are conducted that people would get a dose of encouragement, and advice to faster their career. Once a week within 2-3 hours is good enough. It can also be conducted once a month or biweekly basis, and a long hour to have a detailed discussion. The vital thing is ensuring that the meeting takes place. In the course of the meeting, each member shares their experience at work for that week. The good, bad and ugly, other members see areas where they can help such individual whet their blade and get back on their feet. Each member can cover their experience within 10-15 minutes to give others a chance also to relate their experience. There are individual cases where a member is in a situation where advice, opinion, and guide is needed, and it might require up to an hour brainstorming on the best approach to take. On rare occasions such as this, it might make them more than the regular 2-3 hours. The meetings are brought to a climax with each member mentioning their goal for the week.

Things To Look Out For At The Inception Of A Mastermind

You need a good understanding of a mastermind and know what exactly it is you're looking for before creating one. This knowledge will guide you in certain areas:

The specific value you want from the mastermind

The kind of people you will love to surround yourself

Do you think a mastermind will be advantageous to your career?

After properly evaluating yourself it is imperative that you weigh your options and see if this is really what you want. When it comes to selecting members to make sure you guys have a good connection that will be significant in your professional get. Always be reminded that these people in your group will be a reflection of yourself towards achieving your goals.

Create A Purpose

With a purpose in my mind, it will be easier for you to act and you will be able to determine the type of people you would like to be part of your mastermind. Other criteria still come into play, but the most critical thing is tailoring your purpose with your criteria, that itself is wonderful in achieving results. When people see your plan, and they see the amount of focus on display, it endears them most especially when it is in connection with their profession.

When you're considering people, you vibe with easily, its best to trust your judgment. We've people who at the onset don't open up , but they gradually grow up to become a part of the family. It might be wrong to cast them away at the first point of contact. Either way whoever you choose to bring to your group is a purely subjective decision that is based solely on your judgment.

You need to find a balance between a hard worker and a skillful worker. They are both useful in the mastermind group. Don't let prejudice play a fast one on you by making irrational decisions that could make you lose the true essence of starting a mastermind group.

Create a culture for diversification. Don't be stereotypical by being bent on absorbing people you only share similar goals with. People have varying skill sets, and it's essential that you see beyond the within and see areas where others can also contribute to the development of other members. The employment skills of a business owner can come in handy at the point of hiring a new employee; a sales representative can be useful when you need to sell out your new products. Each of this Personnel have vital contributions that they can make when allowed in the same group. The same with other niches that go beyond management, talk of engineering, art, and digital marketing and a host of others.

A mastermind is a useful productivity tool that helps you stay on top of your profession. It can also be used as a social tool that enables you to maintain a healthy relationship with others which make you socially conscious. The dynamism that it holds makes it even more interesting for people to embrace, you can choose to get creative with it and also get a better result. You don't have to face that struggle of career growth alone, let others help you in making a professional growth.

Chapter 9:
No One Cares About your Brand when you start

I've never been a believer in overnight success. In fact, I've always said there is no formula for success and anybody who makes it look as though it's happened effortlessly in a short period of time, isn't showing the whole picture. While it's not impossible to quickly grow a brand, it's incredibly unlikely and very rarely happens.

The reason? When people haven't grown an attachment to your brand, simply put, they do not yet care. You care as you've put your heart and soul into the brand, dedicating countless hours to perfecting it, but nobody else has the same love for it at the beginning. While family members will always claim they care about the brand, they care more about your own happiness and success, as opposed to actually being attached to the brand itself. They want things to go well for you, and in the majority of cases will be incredibly supportive, whether it's of your business venture or latest hobby. This doesn't mean they won't care about your brand, it only means there is progress still to be made.

Find out your loyal following by setting up a Facebook page for your business, filling out the profile with imagery, brand information, links to websites and any other captivating content you may have.

Next, invite your Facebook friends to like your business page, using the option to invite contacts to visit the page in their masses. In addition to this, you should post on your regular Facebook page, encouraging friends to head over to your business page. The perfect post would be one explaining your latest business venture and why you'd appreciate the support, preferably including imagery or a brand logo to reinforce your message.

This is when it's most important to remember that people don't naturally care about brands instantly. This comes with time, persuasive messaging, exciting products or services and continuous marketing. You may be surprised at how few of your friends like the page, despite previously singing your brand's praises or promising to buy in the future. This mustn't be taken to heart and it doesn't mean they do not support you... this is a common occurrence when starting out in business.

"People don't have the same attachment, passion or love for a brand that a business owner does. This comes with time, marketing and persistence."

Brands = Means to an End

Havas Group's study on Meaningful Brands demonstrated that the majority of consumers are not dedicated to a specific brand. As such, it was found that an enormous 74% of those who use brands would not care at all if the brand completely disappeared from existence. This reinforces the fact that although we may regularly purchase specific brands or products, we are not emotionally connected to these brands, and most of us would not have any issue finding alternative brands.

In addition to this, the same sample stated that of the brands they use, only 27% actually positively impact their lives or wellbeing.

This study was in reference to brands and products which are used daily by consumers, demonstrating an incredibly low brand attachment considering these are everyday items. So why is there so little loyalty to the companies and brands which people use most?

The Marketing Sage's Jeffery Slater spoke about this topic, explaining the reasoning behind lack of brand loyalty. He said: "There is a common misperception by the marketing community that assumes that a consumer cares about a brand. Nothing could be further from the truth. Consumers care about satisfying needs and solving problems. Brands are purely emblematic, vehicles or tools towards something bigger. Consumers love the experience they have through a brand – but it isn't the brand itself that matters. More often than not, it is about being part of community."

In other words, instead of consumers growing a connection with the brand, they associate the brand with the process towards an end goal, or as part of a user base who use a particular product. While a makeup fanatic may not have a strong connection to the Maybelline brand, they may regularly use Maybelline makeup as it aligns with their passion or interests, and many others they know also do the same. As such, the majority of people see brands as a useful source of products of services; a means to an end.

The topic of communities who use brands is commonly debated. The time when people feel most attachment to a specific brand is when they are surrounded by a group of people with the same interest and the same passion for the chosen brand.

In the Havas Group study, it was also noted that those who stated they had the most meaningful attachment to certain brands were also those which had the largest groups of followings, often creating an online, or real-life community. Examples of this would be Apple, Google, Ferrari and Disney, all of which boast an enormous following but also have loyal customers who see themselves as a consumer of this specific brand. The consumers love the brand and are far less likely to transfer to a rival brand as they see it almost as a part of their identity.

Following on from this, new brands with little to no following always struggle to build up a user base who are truly dedicated. Because of this, brands and companies which are in the earlier stages find it most beneficial to clearly demonstrate the value for customers, explaining what they get for their money and offering incentives to take them from the early stages of brand familiarity to acting on their interest and purchasing.

This is arguably one of the most difficult aspects of business, beginning from very little. However, once a business has made it through this stage, it is on its way to becoming a success, remaining at the forefront of consumers' minds through continuous reminders of its existence. Examples of this can be seeing the company logo every time they use their deodorant, or hearing a tag line every time they tune into a specific radio station. Through this alone, the likelihood of purchasing again increases greatly, providing it was a positive experience.

Humans are Creatures of Habit

For decades, a common belief has been that if you provide a better product or better value than a competitor, consumers will choose you over them. As much as I'd love to say this is true, it is nowhere near as simple as this.

Unfortunately, people don't always make decisions based on logic. Our minds work in a way that we fill in any areas we are uncertain about, making quick and spontaneous decisions when it comes to which product or service to choose. Logical decision-making does occur, for example working out which is the better value for money, or which is likely to last longer, but we often make decisions based on spur of the moment choices. This is called processing fluency, where the brain makes a compulsive decision quicker than a person can understand why or how they have come to make their choice. An example of this would be somebody deciding they do not like the taste of cinnamon and as a result of this, opting not to buy a cinnamon scented candle, without even smelling it, based on the memory and assumption that they would not like it. The brain often computes this information so quickly that the individual is not even aware of this thought process.

Processing fluency is a result of repetition, with the brain prioritising what it recognises as being a regular occurrence. Our brain becomes so familiar with places, times, items or brands that alternatives can make us feel uneasy, choosing us to opt for the 'safe' option. If you have drunk Starbucks coffee regularly for the last five years, chances are, when presented with an alternative, you will choose Starbucks over a new coffee you are not familiar with.

Another aspect which goes into decision making during a purchase is social desirability. This automaticity sees us make an assumption based on whether others like the product or service before we try it. Seeing other satisfied customers often does a great job of convincing ourselves we will also be a fan.

These automatically occurring processes see the gap widen between brands or business you know, and unfamiliar ones, regardless of whether they provide the exact same service or not. While this makes it more difficult for a new brand to be chosen, it is not impossible.

Consumers' decisions can still be swayed by particular attributes we find attractive, a change in price, a special offer or an impressive marketing campaign. These reasons make it more than possible for any new brand to become a favourite, albeit the odds are not in favour of this happening.

Simply put, as a new brand, you have to make people care about your brand. People won't easily decide your brand is superior to another and they will need convincing, not only winning them over but making them go against natural brain patterns which tempt them towards what is familiar to them.

How to Make People Care About Your Brand

While I've previously mentioned automaticity, this can also be used in your favour. While people like what is already familiar to them, you can cleverly market a product to still align with their interests.

Many large-scale retailers use targeted advertising to present new brands and opportunities to customers they know have an interest in similar items. For example, somebody who recently purchased a pair of football boots may see a ball and pump in advertising spaces. Using this tailored advertising space to attract the attention of the viewer combines their trust within this sector or area and encourages them to make more purchases, albeit from a new, unfamiliar brand.

Through creating attractive offers related to similar, previously purchased items, online stores and brands have benefited enormously.

Growing sales and customer loyalty through tapping into the themes and interests of viewers is one of the most effective ways to not only capture users' attention, but encourage them to make purchases.

This is a brilliant method of growing customer loyalty through subjects of interest and exposing them to any chosen brand.

To put this into practice, you are able to grow brand awareness and following through tapping into consumers' habits and using these to align with your brand. Creating numerous exposures and interactions between the potential consumer and any brand will close the gap between the brands they currently use and yours. Online, you are able to appear regularly with meaningful messaging and even 24/7, using social media's global reach. While doing this, you are able to work on complex business plans and methods of growing the brand even further.

Social media is a vital tool in current marketing, enabling you to boost your brand's recognition, awareness and reputation easily and quickly with the correct knowledge. So what should you be aiming to achieve on social media?

To grow brand interaction and success, there are endless methods of achieving this on social media. The main aim should be to grow the number of views, comments, likes, shares and engagements as well as clicks which link back to your website, product or further information.

Planning targeted advertising can ensure you reach the correct audience even if they do not interact with the post, meaning they are still becoming more familiar with the brand. Those who do click on calls to action or head over to purchase products can be encouraged to make smaller, less expensive purchases before they opt for larger, more expensive purchases. Using this 'tripwire' method to start small, some of the biggest benefits can be found when getting users to make numerous purchases within a short timescale, continuously reminding them of your products of services.

Creating an online community or forum brings the opportunity to provide top quality customer service, offering advice and support to those who visit. This is one of many ways of encouraging conversation and a positive reputation around your brand. Other ideas include partnering with another successful brand or company, which is not a direct competitor with yourself, working in collaboration with a charity or even searching the App Store for an app which helps you to build customer conversation and dedication surrounding your brand.

Chapter 10:

What is The Digital marketing?

Introduction

Digital marketing can be likened to a Sequoia which serves as an umbrella to every form of electronic channels used for marketing. There have been a growing number of internet users in recent years which has contributed to global outreach marketers are enjoying in the online space. And it's becoming more apparent that people now seldom patronize the traditional paradigm in trading. Who wouldn't love to sit back on their couch and wait for their goods, walk into their homes? That's the sheer amazement that comes with shopping online. But before we move too far, let me give you a simplified definition of digital marketing.

Digital marketing is the application of simple marketing tactics to find potential customers anywhere they might be which mostly is on the internet. There are a lot of tactics used by the marketer to reach out to customers, and everything is captured under the umbrella of digital marketing.

Measures employed by digital marketers

A professional digital marketer understands the impact of a good marketing campaign in creating a better outreach to potential customers. Depending on the scale of the campaign they sometimes employ free and paid channel within their disposal to make the campaign goal-oriented. Here is a real-life scenario of how marketers influence a product, A content marketer can curate a series of blog post about a clothing line the company is about to launch, the social media marketer of the company goes to the company social media accounts and dazzles the product with some cute captions. Finally, the email marketer sends a mail to prospective fashionistas who would love to rock those clothes. And that's how the product gets publicized. We will be digging a little deeper into some tactics employed by digital marketers.

Search Engine Optimization(SEO)

This involves the use of Google's ranking model to get organic traffic on your website. The higher you rank, the better your site gets to the top list of search engines. This approach is beneficial to outlets such as blogs, websites, infographics.

Content Marketing

This requires promoting content in a bid to generate awareness globally for a brand, traffic growth and get customers, all of which are done organically. The outlets that you can use for promoting your content are blog posts, ebooks, and whitepaper, brochures, and infographics.

Social media marketing

This entails the use of different social media platforms as a channel to promote content that will help generate awareness, conversion, and traffic to your website. Channels employed for this are; Google+, Facebook, Twitter, Instagram, LinkedIn, Snapchat, Pinterest and so on.

Pay-per-click (PPC)

Every time there is a click on the link to your website you will pay the publisher. The most common type is the Google AdWords which involves paying Google to feature your link in top search engine website. Other outlets where you can utilize this are; facebook, twitter and LinkedIn.

Affiliate Marketing

This is the process of getting paid by promoting other peoples product on your website. You're indirectly generating leads to their page. You can use the following outlets; posting links on your social media platforms, using the hosting of video ads on YouTube.

Native Advertising

This approach is primarily content-oriented where you feature content on a platform, and other non paid content. A simplified example is the BuzzFeed post, and some are of the opinion that posting content on

73

social media page like Facebook also counts.

Marketing Automation

This involves the use of software to help automate posting on social media platforms without having to carry out repetitive tasks manually. Most organizations employ this method to make posts without such as email newsletter, social media posts, lead generation workflows, campaign updates.

Email Marketing

Several organizations use this method to reach out to their audience to pass information concerning the firm. In some cases used to give information about an upcoming event, drive the attention of customers to their mail or social media platforms. The types of email you might send varies and mostly depends on what you're planning on achieving. We have examples such as; follow up emails, welcome emails, newsletter, and so on.

Online PR

This is a form of engagement with your clients, followers with the use of contents, blog post, digital publication. It is akin to the traditional PR we are used to, but it is done within the online space. They use outlets such as; social media, comment section on blogs/website and a host of others.

Inbound Marketing

This is an approach that is specifically tailored to potential customers that will bring returns to the organization by engaging and delighting customers with the use of contents. You can use every digital measure outlined above in the inbound pattern of marketing.

The primary function of digital marketers

There are two things every organization wants from a digital marketer which are brand awareness and lead generation with the use of all digital channels which mostly are social media platforms. One such outlet is the SEO ranking which helps companies generate organic traffic to their page. Other channels are companies own websites, blogs, emails, and so on. Digital marketers use different key performance indicators to measure the performance of different channels of marketing. Depending on how big an organization is, responsibility such as digital marketing is usually delegated to different individuals based on which of the digital marketing tools they are skilled at using.

But in some cases, a small company might employ a single digital marketer to take all of these responsibilities. Here are some critical specialties of digital marketers;

SEO manager (key performance indicator: organic traffic)

They work with content creators to get content that will rank on google search with a good topic and keywords. Some of which might be posted on the company social media page.

Content Marketer (key performance indicators: blog traffic, time on page, YouTube subscribers)

They work with other departments in the organization to ensure all of the companies information outlets is not drab. They sometimes back up the content with videos to make the platform more engaging. Once any new products come from the company, they find a way to pitch it to the client via their social media and the company's website.

Social Media Personnel (key personal indicators: likes, follows, impressions)

A social media personal oversees the activities of a company on their social media page. He is saddled with the responsibility of posting scheduled content on the social media page it could be visual or written. Whichever platform they use is dependent on the company they work for. They Sometimes relate with the content marketer about possible content that should be posted on a page.

Marketing Automation manager (Key performance indicator: conversion rate, campaign click, email opening.

This individual manages and checks the performs of the software used for implementing the automated task of posting content on social media platforms or websites. This is an excellent tool to gauge the performance of the campaign of the company.

It is vital that each organization have someone to checklist their performance on individual platforms, this is the best approach to measure the level of progress of their campaign, traffic, conversion rate and so on.

The difference between inbound and digital marketing

Most people have a misconstrued idea of what each of these stands for and not that am blaming them, and it's quite easy to misjudge what they stand for especially from the surface. They both depend on the internet, and both require content so where is the contrast. Digital marketing is a sequoia to both the inbound and outbound system of marketing. Where the digital outbound, is inclined towards reaching out to a large number of people about a brand whether it's beneficial to them or not. Digital inbound functions otherwise, it involves the use of digital marketing tools to pitch your product to people who seem interested in them or who the product might beneficial to.

Both the inbound and outbound sits under the shed of digital marketing, primarily utilizing it tools for a campaign, brand awareness, and whatnot.

Does every business require digital marketing?

Every organization needs the input of a digital marketing outlet to create brand awareness. Regardless of what you sell or your type of service you need to build your customer base by channeling content that appeals to the persona of your potential customers. This is not

77

implying that every business should employ a similar approach when carrying out campaigns with the aid of digital marketing tools. Examples of some business model approach towards digital marketing:

B2B Digital Marketing Tools

If your organization is built on the business to business framework, then your digital marketing approach will be tailored towards getting high profiled organization which will end up getting in touch with your salesperson. In cases such as this, your campaign needs to be highly professional and engaging. Asides from keeping your website active, you will find your prospective clients waiting on social media platforms such as LinkedIn.

B2C Digital Marketing Tools

If the operation of your business is built on this framework then what you're looking for is finding a way to engage your prospective customers to your website instead of speaking to a salesperson. Then you have to be with your clients digitally up till the point when that product leaves their cart and gets checked out. You need active verbs in your content, a call to action message that turns every click into a conversion.

Benefits of digital marketing

Let's be realistic, the traditional approach towards carrying out advertisement can be no way compared to the results that digital marketing brings. You can even measure your ROI and pinpoint which of the outlet led to the traffic you have. If you've ever placed an advert on a newspaper, you would agree how painstaking it is to get a single person check that page and make an effort in purchasing your product. Compared to digital marketing, I will say the traditional marketing is a complete waste of resource. Let's see some examples of how digital marketing is of use to every business and organization.

Organic Traffic

There are digital analytics tools that can give you real-life figures of the number of people that visited your page, location, the type of platform and a host of other information. All of these you're not opened to with the use of the traditional marketing tools. If you check the analytics tool and see that Facebook generated a good number of traffic to your website, then you can invest more on the platform. It also helps you study the pattern of behavior of your clients to see how they react towards your products and see how you can improve on your online store to help them make purchases.

Content and lead generation

You've taken out time to curate an article, and you posted in a newspaper column, with the intent of getting people to read and further publicize your content. But in the actual sense, it will be difficult for you to measure this outcome since there is no way to know the number of people who flipped through that page, not to mention reading through your content. But the narratives are very different with digital marketing, imagine posting that same content on your website you can check the number of people who read the article and also get the emails of those who downloaded the content by filling the form section.

Attribution model

This is another useful digital marketing tool which helps you trace your customers point of contact with your business. This tool is helpful in that it helps you to know which channel is to get credit for the success of a campaign. It gives you a broad perspective of how people knew about your product and the process of purchase. Primarily this is one of the most useful tools that help you make a healthy business decision. You will know which of the digital outlet if functional and where you need to invest, areas to work on an outlet you need to cut out.

What kind of content should I create on my digital platforms?

It is essential that you connect with your buyers and the only way is through your content. Ensure you tailor your content to their needs and see how you can make something out of your possible narrative. At the point of creating the content, you might need to do a handful of research through the use of content mapping. It is a form of a mental walk through into what would make your buyer patronize you. When it comes to the right kind type of content to post on your page it goes in stages, and we will outline each of them:

Awareness stage:

Blogs

Once you have suitable material that is SEO enabled with the great use of keywords, then you're one step away from generating organic traffic to your blog.

Infographics

This is one effective way of creating awareness for your brands and business by sharing these images on social media platforms.

Short videos

Visual aids are quite easy to win people over especially when it is handled professionally. You can post videos on YouTube or host them through an influencer and watch your brand gets the right amount of recognition.

Consideration stage:

EBooks are useful tools for getting leads and can be more effective than a blog post.

A research report is also valid for generating leads especially when it backed up with statistics.

Webinars are useful tools because it is interactive and holds more depth of information.

Decision stage :

• A case study is one way to show potential customers, the pragmatic side of the item of purchase, for those who are geared towards making a purchase this is one way to drive them to your side.

• Testimonials are a good way of showing how much your success your product have recorded or how those who purchased it are finding it compelling.

When do I start getting the result of my digital marketing?

With digital marketing getting results for your campaign is way more comfortable and it happens at the fastest rate. As long as you have taken out time to do a smart content mapping, then you have no problem getting your result at least within six months. But if it is a paid digital advert, then you can your result quickly.

What should be my budget if I want to run a digital campaign?

This lies solely on the type of approach you're planning on using. If it's the inbound technique which involves using SEO ranking, social media platform, content marketing and so on, you might not need a huge budget especially if you're planning a DIY strategy. But for the outbound technique where you might need to purchase emails and contact information for cold calls, you might need a substantial budget for that.

Importance of mobile device in digital marketing

Research shows that 69% of people in united states spend a good number of time enjoying digital marketing, even desktop usage doesn't account for less. People are so attached to their mobile device making it the first point of contact with digital marketing. Whenever you're creating your website ensure it is mobile user-friendly, so that client can engage with you on the go. Ensure all social media, and digital campaign is mobile friendly this will help accrued more customers than the traditional desktop platform.

I know you can't wait to take your market to the next point of sale and this material has been tailored towards helping you achieve that. If you've been into digital marketing for a while and still not getting needed result, then it is time to consider other areas of digital marketing that can help revamp your digital trading experience.

Chapter 11:
Future of Ecommerce

If ecommerce is at its infancy, it means the road ahead is pretty open for more players to show innovation and claim more cuts. That also means that as Amazon turns 25 with 37% of global ecommerce market control; a projection by Sellbrite estimates that the retail conglomerate would responsible for half of the ecommerce sales in three years, meaning more opportunities exist for competition to show innovation and set new records of performance in the industry.

Already, more innovations are being recorded, from two-hour delivery to drone service; the future of ecommerce will continue to excite industry watchers and players knowing key market opportunities and potential points of friction.

Understanding the future of ecommerce with 10 trends that offer the answer

1. Ecommerce Is Growing But at 11.9% of Retail
2. Multi-Channel Ecommerce Enables Anywhere Buying
3. Ecommerce Automation Is an Accessible Reality
4. Mobile Is trending but Adds Purchase Complexities
5. Native Social-Selling Is Finally Delivering Results
6. International Ecommerce Remains Largely Untapped
7. Micro-Moments Are the New Battleground for Optimization

8. Content Is the King of Ecommerce Engagement
9. B2B Ecommerce Dwarfs B2C by Over $5 Trillion
10. Fragmentation Is E-commerce's Biggest Challenge

For the best insights continue reading to understand the big picture trends defining the future of ecommerce:

1. Ecommerce is growing at only 11.9% of retail sales

The estimate of 2018 ecommerce percentage market share of retail sales will increase to 11.9% from 3.5% over a year ago; this shows brick and mortar business still maintains its dominance by a massive margin.

This shows that the future of ecommerce is bright with more opportunities for players. However, business who wants to grow need to continually watch the market, innovate and improve in-store experiences at every touch point of ecommerce expressions.

How?

It is evident that ecommerce and offline partnerships are possible where an ecommerce store opens a brick and mortar storefronts to breathe physical life into a digital experience. An example is the retail giants YM Inc, a brick and mortar with online to offline experience. This idea brings into play the word omnichannel. For more in-depth understanding, research content on Omni-Channel Retailing;

2. Multi-channel ecommerce enables anywhere buying

This is the art and science of decoding the reasons why customers buy your product across different channels of selling. It requires finding opportunities in your data, and creatively positions your business to sell on a budget when the opportunity arises. However, it's about creating a balance and understanding when and where to amplify or show restraint in your channel mix, to not overwhelm your following or burn your resources to convert people who are not interested.

Multi-channel ecommerce needs proper setup and maintain adequate inventory management system; otherwise selling using this method can be futile. Equally, you need multi-channel attribution to measure results. The challenge in this, however, is that its success depends on consolidating the multiple channels into one system. Many retailers lack this requirement, and it is difficult to achieve inventory visibility across stores, vendors, and warehouse to serve multi-channel adequately.

Therefore, to survive and thrive in the future of ecommerce, there is a need for store infrastructure to manage and maintain automated multichannel retailing with minimal manual input.

3. Ecommerce automation is an accessible reality

Would you tell anyone, if your business had the secret to save time, lower costs and sell more?

Giant enterprises who had this secret a decade never shared with anyone; the Amazon, Walmart, and Costco had the early lead because of their access to resources not available to other, they took advantage of it without letting anyone into the secret. However, today, we know that secret to be marketing automation!

For the future of emerging ecommerce, the new secret is automation.

Staying tight-lipped on this secret was a phenomenon for the forefront entrepreneurs; not even Google Trends was able to dig deep.

Of course, we should understand the reason for the silence which are in two parts: the first reason is that no ecommerce offered comprehensive automation as an accessible feature; the second reason is that businesses that automate did so in-house at huge costs or went into a joint venture on mix-and-match workaround using a third-party application.

However, at Shopify Plus, three tools are unleashing ecommerce automation:
1. Shopify Flow
It's a three-step visual builder helping to automate any customer-facing or back-office process you want. This is done by specifying triggers, conditions, and actions; to do this, it requires download and installs some ready-made workflows, done entirely without coding.

2.   Launchpad

This is a command center for major ecommerce activities including flash sales, product releases, and special events. This ecommerce resource takes away the heavy lifting and guesswork off your shoulders by scheduling everything on your to-do-list preparatory for the big day of your event; just sit back and rake revenue to your store with absolute ease!

3.   Shopify Scripts

With this third tool, you can add automatic discounts, related pay options, and custom shipping options to create excellent checkout experience per customer. It gives you fine-grain control over the customer's cart; this is one way to reduce abandoned cart at checkout point and make more money through sales throughput!

These tools when implemented for your ecommerce can save time, lower cost, boost selling with secure automation system at your fingertip!

4.   Mobile is trending but adds purchase complexities

Mobile traffic is increasing at a phenomenal rate, outpacing desktop traffic almost twice in volume. Data from Adobe shows 46% to 36% traffic volumes for mobile and desktop respectively in 2017. The exciting part is that out of the 46% of traffic from mobile devices, only 30% of it resulted in sales.

The report further shows that people browse on mobile but prefer to buy on the desktop; however, Shopify recorded mobile sales volume of 64% of BFCM resulting in 10% above previous year.

What could be responsible for Shopify beating the established ecommerce mobile conversion rate by twice? The answer lies in the fact that all Shopify stores mobile friendly. It means that the approach to mobile ecommerce design and optimization favors mobile conversion.

Only websites that are mobile friendly will offer user experience on mobile platforms and take them through sales without confusion. a site may be mobile friendly, but without being mobile payment friendly, it will not offer customers the flexibility to checkout successfully.

One of Shopify mobile payment design, Shopify Pay, offers 3x faster payment on mobile which customers find easier for checkout.

To achieve the checkout speed to make mobile users comfortable, ecommerce players need to invest in new payment technologies and have a checkout design that gives users the confidence and trust to check out. Right now, the average mobile user understands the fragile security nature of mobile devices, unless the ecommerce site can guarantee better experience, customers will be scared to use it. Even Google won't readily allow its email account users to open their emails on phones without initial warning.

Therefore, ecommerce that want the Shopify experience need to deplore more efforts to deliver quality mobile payment experience for consumers.

5.   Native social-selling is finally delivering results

We can all attest to the overwhelming influence of social media with 3 out of every adult in cities with access to internet having a social media account. If you meet an adult with a social media account, the possibility of having two other accounts from other platforms is 98% which they visit daily.

According to Flurry, average digital adult spends up to five hours per day on their chosen social media with interest in social networking, chatting, messaging, or entertainment. And some do buy products and services too when they see product the caught their attention; a 2016 survey supports this with 18.2% respondent claiming they bought products directly on social media

Social influencer marketing is multimillion dollars businesses of helping brands convert consumers for sales. Celebrities are making cool money with product endorsement thanks for large followers, likes and comments they have on their chosen social media that ecommerce and even brick and mortar businesses are leveraging to boost sales.

Ecommerce enterprises and even brick and mortar businesses are finding usefulness for Instagram, Facebook, and Pinterest. Enterprises like ORO LA increased its monthly revenue up to 29.3% using

Instagram. The result is more amazing when you combined an increase in your mobile results with social media success for your business; think about it!

6.   International ecommerce remains largely untapped

Global ecommerce potentials owe tremendous opportunities for enterprises who understand what it takes to tap into the market. McKinsey says the global middle-class citizen would grow by 1.4 billion people by 2020 as expected; the Asia Pacific region will account for 85% of the new entrant into the middle-class rank.

Already, some enterprises with insights are making a move to tap into the opportunity; an example in this instance is the William Wrigley Jr. Company with 40% market share in China for his chewing gum product.

Enterprise leaders with foresight would struggle to take advantage of the international opportunities offered by ecommerce. Country by country, enterprises will need to observe carefully before entering because each market presents unique constraints, preferences and security issues.

One thing is evident regarding the future of ecommerce – the opportunity will be there, the constraints will also be there, and this calls for innovation on the part of every enterprise to overcome any challenge and seize the opportunity. The ecommerce that can find a way around a perceived difficulty will be the winner. A case in this regard is Shopify who achieved higher mobile sales through enhanced mobile payment

Companies who were able to eliminate market risks in Africa are today making huge sales without the risk like the Mall for Africa strategy that helps bring US and UK products to Nigeria and other African countries to reduce risk and achieve their sales goal. You can consider a better way to penetrate a market without exposing yourself to the dangers.

7.   Micro-moments are the new battleground for optimization
Ecommerce has eliminated the concept of one-size-fits-all marketing. To remain competitive in a digital business environment; marketing efforts are towards micro-moments to address individual customer's needs rather than generalized advertising to sell your product to potential customers.

Micro-moments features:
- In-the-moment buying choices
- Decisions to resolve problems immediately
- Decisions to try out new things in routine moments
- The pursuit of big goals during downtime

Never in business history has the concept of the customer as the king been brought to this level of implementation as ecommerce demands. Every customer bound communication must be personalized and optimized including transactional messages such as emails for purchase confirmation, shipping notification, and status updates. Transactional messages help to boost repeat sales, build loyalty and deepen engagement with the customer.

While all other messages may end up in the spam box, rarely will transactional messages be missed because a buyer is excited to get an update from the seller. Confident your transactional emails would get opened, ensure to engage with the following types of optimizations:

- Cross-sells based on seasonality and purchase
- How-to videos and buying guides
- Links to your mobile app
- Exclusive offers

When sending out transactional emails, you can include any upsell information that will lead to further engagement and sales while you have the attention of your customer.

8.   Content is the king of ecommerce engagement

Content is king; you can understand this against the belief that content is educational, entertaining, and helpful for customers to build their knowledge base about your product and services. By informing your customers, you give them the opportunity to make an informed decision.

Content marketing is a cost-effective way to increase your business engagement cost-effectively and impactful ROI. When you rely on strategic content marketing, it helps to save over $14 per new customer you acquired.

While content creation is an essential business tool, creating content takes resources to build a platform to deliver the content and develop the strategy to provide high quality and engaging content to your target audience.

Here is why you need high-quality content:
• Quality content earns you a following from your target audience on social media;
• According to Gartner, 64% of people say that, in their choice of brand, customer experience is more important than price point;
• According to HubSpot, marketers that prioritize blogging are 13 times likely to generate a positive ROI;
• HubSpot says content can double a sites conversion rate.

Content creation may sound so easy; it does require knowing how it's done to deliver quality content and not hurt your website. When creating your content, make sure quality and interactive; only engaging content will provide all the impressive gains alluded to content as a marketing tool. When your content is engaging, the conversion would be excellent!

9.   B2B Ecommerce Dwarfs B2C by Over $5 Trillion

In 2017, Statista says the business volume of B2B ecommerce projection amounts to 7.66 trillion United States dollars. If you are ignoring the business potentials in a B2b ecommerce opportunity before now, it's time to start thinking how to tap into the potential business it offers. This figure amounts to increase of 1.83 trillion US dollars from 2013 B2B business volume projection; the difference is 0.313 trillion to be equal to the volume of business projection for B2C ecommerce in 2017 which was put at $2.143 trillion.

The survey also reported the average rate of conversion for B2B to be 10% while that of B2C was 3%. Targeting B2B market is not without its challenges as they are also likely a B2C shopper on a platform like Amazon who may expect fast, direct and streamlined services without restrictions; usually, they prefer buying from your website, rather than have your sales representative sell to them.

For you to tap into the B2B ecommerce market, there is a need to try and learn how it works along the way.

10.   Fragmentation Is E-commerce's Biggest Challenge

Ecommerce success is also its albatross! Today, consumers have better access to the internet with more power to buy wherever they are. This means the average consumers have the tools to access more retailers ever than before. However, this immediately presents its challenge of exponential access points refers to as touchpoints!

Ecommerce presents both big and small entrepreneurs the same opportunity produce and sell to the same market. While big brands still have their respect in the market, they cannot prevent the small businesses access to the market. The barriers to market entry and exist are gone.

However, the marketing crowd created by free access to the global consumer is a challenge that requires more creativity and innovation to overcome for every ecommerce. As a result, there is an opportunity to win or lose, whether startup or big brand.

Therefore, fragmentation is depicted by consumer behavior and market response. There exists a wider variety among consumers now than before in both developed and emerging markets. While the traditional middle market is shrinking, the top and emerging markets hold the potentials for growth.

The fragmentation notwithstanding, it offers a significant opportunity at the point where the playing field becomes level:

Consumers' media usage is also fragmented with the rise of digital content and the proliferation of online devices. From the Web to mobile, and social sites to radio, TV, and print, each channel has unique requirements, audience appeal, and economics, needing specialized attention. Be that as it may, media campaigns need to be carefully coordinated for effective consumer messaging.

The future of ecommerce, really, lies in the decisions you make to continue to adapt and follow many disruptions that will support many micro and macro decisions that will be made in the effort to reach the consumers every minute!

Chapter 12:

What is the E-Commerce ?

Introduction

It is vital that we establish the meaning of e-commerce before moving too far on this e-commerce train. And it is just any form of buying and selling that takes place on the internet, so if by chance you've purchased or sold something on the internet then you've taken part in e-commerce. Here is a little background story which marked the start of e-commerce. In the middle of 1994, the first-ever online trading was recorded which was done by Phil Brandenberger. He used his credit card to purchase "Ten Summoners' Tales" from strings for $12.48 including shipping fee. Although this story might not be of importance to you, it sure marked the beginning of online trade, and it started right in the beautiful state of Philadelphia. For most this transaction serves as the commencement of the system of trade which we enjoy today and has reached every nook and cranny of the universe.

At the moment e-commerce is getting massive recognition from every part of the world, and global statistics have indicated that there will be a more extensive outreach, come 2020. According to e-market platform, statistics suggest that by 2020 the retail section of e-commerce would have reached a whopping sum of $29 billion. One can compare e-commerce to wine, it gets better with age year in year out there is always growth.

Undoubtedly, e-commerce is enjoying massive success rate in the commerce industry which made it create a bit of interest in you and so many others. Most people see e-commerce as an enigma which has in some way heightened their curiosity. If you're eager like most to jump into this market space, then you need to a comprehensive guide on how best to thrive in online trading. This material has been created for your use, to provide a profound understanding of the e-commerce space – its inception, what it entails, a platform where you can trade either as a buyer or seller, gimmicks that can help you to succeed. Whether you're a newbie or you've been in the e-commerce trade for sometimes look no further you've found yourself on the right path. You will read firsthand stories of merchants, not just their breakthroughs but that which almost made them give up on their struggle. Come on along as we unravel the secrets that make a successful merchant in the online market.

Categories of online merchants

There are three major categories of online merchants, and they're grouped according to the following criteria; what, whom, and where they trade. We will take a look at each category which will give us a better understanding of the types of the e-commerce platform that we have.

According to what they sell

We will be considering e-commerce merchants first based on the products they have for sale on their online store.

1.   Online stores with general items

These are stores that sell fashion items and household products, especially products that are used on a regular basis. These retailers display their products on their webpage, and they give customers the opportunity to make their selection which is kept in their cart. Once payment is done, the retailers deliver the product down to the preferred location of the client. Some retailers are putting up an avenue through which clients can come pick up their items within the store. We have a lot of online stores with fashion and household items; for example, Alibaba sells a wide range of household products, Mr porter sells males apparel which includes clothes, shoes, bags and so on.

2.   Retailers with service-based platforms

Freelancing is gradually becoming a household name, and it implies that you don't have to be available in person before you can render some essential services which range from teaching, consulting and so on. They have platforms where you can request their services and get your job done as quick as possible. One such platform is upwork; a hub for professionals where you offer services based on your skillset and get paid for it.

3. Digital markets

E-commerce is a digitally enabled process, and its operation is solely based on the concept. Retailers sell digital products on the internet such as eBooks, online courses, stock photos and so on. The internet has brought new dawn where you can be seated comfortably in the corner of your home and taking professional courses. You can go as far as learning vocational skills right on the internet, no doubt it's a global village with profound advantage. Merchants such as Pixabay provides you with stock images; you can learn vocational skills and professional courses from Lynda.com. You're opened to a wide range of opportunities when you utilize a platform such as this.

According to the type of merchants involved

This is another way in which we can categorize e-commerce, there are several merchants involved in online trading but with a different mode of operation. Here are the types of traders in the online market:

1. Business to consumer (B2C)

It is a form of transaction that takes place between a seller and the consumer of the product. This implies that business directly transacts with the end user of the item which always happens to be the consumer. Their mode of transaction is purely based on this model. Stores such as Zappos, Modcloth, nasty gal and so on, sells to the final consumer.

2. Business to business (B2B)

This type of model involves a transaction between two companies where one company provides services to the other. When you hear of organizations that render services for other business, it means they operate on a business to business platform. The popular B2B platform is square a firm that offers accounting solution to small-scale/mid-size businesses.

3. Consumer to business (C2B)

This is a setup in which a consumer contributes either through monetary or service rendered to a company. Companies get crowdfunding from consumers through the initial public offering, and this might be for starting a project, or the development of the company. Crowdsourcing is nothing new in the business sector. Brands such as Patagonia, Oreo, Pepsi uses this model to achieve specific projects.

4. Consumer to consumer (C2C)

This type of business model is popular since it takes place on a daily basis between customers. You purchase a product and can choose to sell it off to another consumer. Platforms such as eBay and craigslist offer consumers the opportunity to resell old items to other consumers.

5. Government to Business (G2B)

In this scenario, the business is purchasing a product from the government via the internet. It might be the payment of a levy, office space, services which is paid online. In different parts of the world, citizens are charged for taxes, bills, mortgage by the government online.

6.   Business to Government (B2G)

This type of e-commerce involves the purchase of an item or payment for a service, paid for by the government to a company. Consider a company which develops software that helps the government monitor the productivity of their staff, after the service has been completed then the government pays via the internet that is a business to government e-commerce.

7.   Consumer to Government (C2G)

Consumers pay for taxes, bills, parking ticket via the internet which is a form of e-commerce. If you pay for parking tickets and other levy mandated by the authority of your location, then you fall into this category.

During this write-up, we've outlined the type of transaction that takes in the online store. We will take a keen look into platforms where e-commerce takes place and how they happen.

1.   An Online Store

With an online store, the merchant creates a website and post their product on the page. This undoubtedly is a straightforward approach to pitching your product to customers while finding a solution to their shopping needs. We have curated a list of top rated online sellers that can provide real solutions to your shopping needs.

• Magento

This e-commerce friendly platform offers a cutting-edge solution to merchants. They have the freedom to create a customized space that fits perfectly to the need of their product. You will also have access to their support team to get first-hand help; they also get you connected to other merchants on their platform. You can further enhance your trade with the use of add-ons.

• Demandware

Demandware is an e-commerce solution company that gives you the cloud space to make your trade. You won't have to go through the hurdle of creating or maintaining your page since the company takes care of these (although this might hold you back in certain areas). One advantage Demandware holds over it contemporaries is helping merchants to sell across the board, without limiting them to a particular channel.

• Oracle Commerce

As merchandise with an array of products, the right avenue for you is oracle commerce. A place where you can sell from simple to complex products. For merchandise that operates on B2B and B2C transactions, this is the right platform for you. One of its amazing features is the ability for merchandise to customize their products to whatever taste they desire.

- Shopify

This is the abode for small and medium scale businesses. You can sell your product physically and with digital aids. Using Shopify is pretty easy and requires no special computer skills. They come with features that can help you manage your sales inventory such as reporting, inventory management, buy button and a host of others. For those who use social media apps like Facebook and Pinterest, you can take advantage of their social selling features.

- Woocommerce

If you're a WordPress user, then you shouldn't sleep on the cool advantage Woocommerce brings to you. It's a user-friendly platform that comes with tools that enhances your success rate as a merchant, tools such as analytics, reporting, shipping options and a host of others. The good thing is each of these features is user-friendly. It is solely meant for WordPress users alone since the platform connects effortlessly with WordPress.

- BigCommerce

Small and large-scale businesses can use this platform for sales. You will not be cornered to a particular outlet, and your products can go on social media platforms as well as sites like Amazon, ebay, google shopping and so on. They also accommodate merchants with B2B transactions whether they're selling to other business or wholesalers. The platform is fully maintained by the administrator so that you're focused on what is essential which is making huge returns on your products.

- Volusion

A popular e-commerce platform that allows merchandise post their products and get paid all on the same platform. It contains mouthwatering features that bring suitable solutions to your online trading needs. The features are marketing tools, shopping cart software, and so on.

- Drupal Commerce

The Drupal commerce operates as an open source framework which permits merchandise to set up their online store and apps. Merchandise on this platform is productive with their sales due to it core modules which enhances their trade. Another popular platform is commerce kickstart, a product of drupal commerce but comes with trading tools that help merchandise launch their store at a faster rate.

2. Online Trading space

Online trading spaces are sites that offer space for merchandise to display their products. It is vital to establish that most online stores don't own the product on their page, what they do is connect the buyer to the seller. They are only offering an avenue for merchandise to sell their product. Here are popular online trading spaces on the internet:

- Amazon

For a fact, Amazon have grown to become a household name with a wide range of product on their site. Some of the products include clothing, books, fashion accessories, and so much more. The yearly turn over on Amazon is evident that e-commerce has become widely accepted. Third-party sellers made as much as $2billion in the year 2015.

- eBay

eBay stands as the most versatile of the online trading space which allows different forms of transactions such as B2B, B2C, C2C. They've varieties of products such as clothes, fashion accessories, electronic gadgets, and so on. Merchants have the privilege of conducting auctions, through which customers bid for a certain product and the agreeable price might even surpass the market value.

- Etsy

An online trading spaces with special types of goods. This space is meant for innovators who generate independent finances through their creation. People love this platform because of the collective spirit and oneness of selling custom-made products.

- Alibaba

Whether you import or export, wholesaler, retailer Alibaba accommodates all. Merchandise can purchase in bulk and resell at a suitable price. One can say conclusively, that Alibaba is a home for all.

- Fivver

This has been a source of outreach for service providers to get in touch with people who might be in need of their services. In some cases, the price of service could go as far as thousands of dollars, but the minimum amount starts from $5. You can find services such as blog writing, graphics designing, web creation and a host of others.

• Upwork

This is a professional marketplace that connects service providers to those that needs it. The services provided on upwork are versatile, but most importantly they're professional. They include writers, designers, consultants, video assistant and so on.

3.   Social media

This plays a fundamental role in helping merchandise make sales by displaying their product on either Facebook or Pinterest. There are two ways in which social network helps merchandise to grow their customer base. The first involves directing buyers to the merchant's online store. While the second involves helping the buyer purchase directly from the merchant.

How social media spurn the interest of the buyer

Sellers post their products on either of facebook, twitter, Instagram or Pinterest. Any of these avenues can be used by sellers to display their product. It is essential to note that you only pitch your product indirectly to the client, which they can later to check out your link to see your product. Some sellers who use Instagram for making sales use apps such as like2buy to provide access to their link, if the clients are interested wants to purchase their product.

Turning every click to a conversion on social media

You can get every click on your social media page purchasing your product. How have social media been able to evolve up till this point? There have been specific development in some instances, take for example Pinterest introduced the buying features that keep customers on the site without having to direct them to the e-commerce site. Shopify made use of something similar to Facebook where you can purchase a product without leaving the Shopify store. Although, there are downturns experienced by some social sites in implementing this such as the case of Twitter. They had to shut down the whole project in 2014.

The Highs and lows of e-commerce platform

At this junction, we will outline the success story of specific e-commerce site and the downturn of some e-commerce platform.

The high story of e-commerce space

• Amazon

Amazon has permeated every nook and cranny of digital sales spreading its tentacles at a high rate, and it is being regarded as the most successful e-commerce site in the world. In his new book Be like Amazon: even a lemonade can stand to do it, author, Bryan Eisenberg mentions four key areas that helped Amazon stayed prolific.

1.   They have built a system of operation around the need of their client.

2.   Staying innovative have made them beat the expectations of their client continually.

3.   Amazon is far more concerned about keeping their customers, and they do these by offering them a lifetime experience.

4.   They utilize the raw data they have to improve the effectiveness of their page giving it a dark feeling.

The downturn story of an e-commerce site

* Boo.com

This is a UK store that crashed out two years after it launched and this is due to poor business decisions.

To run the site effectively needed javascript and some heavy files which led to the system lagging behind and continuously brought about bad user experience for customers. Another considerable pitfall is at the point where they decided to expand their webpage, and they couldn't come up with the expenses it entails, so they had to lose it all.

Bring your e-commerce knowledge and experience into fruition

The e-commerce space is large and wide enough for everyone to thrive and it is very much possible to achieve this and a whole lot more. We've outlined steps that can guide you when making an informative decision on your e-commerce site. Ensure you take one or two lessons from Amazon and boo.com. It gives you a foregleams of what you need to do and how best to go about it. Continue to remain prolific in your business and find ways to get better.

Chapter 13:
What is dropshipping?

Introduction

Dropshipping is a form of retailing mechanism where a retailer doesn't offer stock products in their store. And this is carried out by getting the product from a third-party seller, and the retailer gets it shipped down to the buyer. In this case, the seller might not have physical contact with the product before passing it across to the required location. The difference between this system of retailing and the conventional mode of retailing is that goods will not be kept. They get the products from a wholesaler or the manufacturer and sells to the consumer. What this implies, is that you don't need to have a stockpile of goods before you can partake in dropshipping.

There are numerous benefits attached to this model of trading which has always made it a top-shelf option for startups and developed business. However, certain drawbacks come with using dropshipping. We will discuss each of the benefits and disadvantages that come with using the model of trading.

Benefits of dropshipping

Small capital business

The biggest of the advantage that endears merchant to this mode of trading, it that little or no capital is required in some instances. As a merchant, you're not obligated to store up products before you can start making earnings. This removes the laden of searching for loans before you can venture into a trade. The conventional approach to retail traders is finding a location and getting it stocked up with your product of choice. You can indulge in business without going through the hurdles of purchasing items that might require intense financial commitment. It is possible to get your first capital from your earnings on a product sold. You can start making early returns with dropshipping since you're neither buying the product as a retailer nor manufacturing the product.

Less stress in establishing

To start a virtual business is way easier to achieve than selling physical products. There are things you won't be concerned about which naturally might be a hindrance in starting your establishment. Things such as:

- Delivering your orders
- Tracking shipping orders
- Paying for a physical store or warehouse
- Making refunds on inbound products or some damages
- Taking accurate records of sales and shipping

You can conserve your energy and save yourself the stress of packing, stacking, and storing up products. Naturally being a retailer comes with serious heavy lifting and it becomes daunting when you don't have anyone to come to your aid. Your best option is to embrace drop shipping where the supplier of the products handles most of the responsibilities. As a retailer, there are things you can indulge in that will aid the growth of your business other than stockpiling goods. And that's where drop shipping puts you ahead of your contemporaries. You have the mental energy to think and see ways to take your business to a whole new level. What most retailers don't know is that having a good customer relationship will aid the growth of your business. That should be your primary focus if you're using dropshipping as your model of trade.

Low expenditure

You're free from the cost of paying for a store or warehouse. Your focus will be tailored towards generating revenues to develop your trade. People start as little as their garage before they get to the point where they grow and have inventory to store in warehouses. But for most small and medium scale business it is advised to find a place in your home where you can make your trade until it gets to the point where you can get a space. There are business thriving which started with a meager amount, and some could go as low as $100. They were able to achieve this because they used their homes as their office space, all they needed was a computer to assist them in keeping a good record. As merchandise, this affords you the opportunity of spending more time with your family while still earning from your business.

Businesses have faced pitfalls such as a complete closedown due to poor financial decisions by its owners. Collecting big loans to start a trade might be the start of the wreckage of the business, unavoidable circumstances such as unexpected losses can occur and could plunge your business into financial mayhem. But with a trade that requires little or no capital will put you in a safer spot. You're not compelled to make upfront purchase of products.

Flexibility

A merchant that uses this mode of operation can be regarded as a freelancer; your work is remote. You have the freedom over your own time and can be in many places at the same time. All that is required is a stable internet connection that helps you keep tab with your suppliers and customers. It is vital that you maintain a certain degree of closeness with your supplier since they're the holders of the product. With all of these measures in place, you can successfully manage your products regardless of your location.

Most people ditch 9-5 because of its spiraling effect on the bond of family. There are instances where you miss events that matter most to your children, or you leave them to be catered for a different person. Gradually and unnoticeably you're losing whatever bond of friendship you might have built with your family. This and many more have made drop shipping on the bucket list of most people because of its flexibility. Imagine the sheer amazement of staying right in the corner of your room and getting a return on your investment while spending excellent time with your loved ones. Dropshipping recognizes the importance of family bond and offers you the privilege to spend quality with them.

An extensive amount of products

Using drop shipping gives you the privilege to keep your customers engaged by keeping your online space active with varieties of product. And that's the advantage you will have as a retailer using this medium. You will never be cornered into what you should sell. There is no limit to what you can achieve with your business with dropshipping. Consider this scenario, a person who sells apparel in a small space will not be able to accommodate new products due to space. But a person that owns a digital space has room for as much as product as possible, and they can effectively manage them. Since you're not compelled to purchase the product, you can display as much as it pleases you on your online space.

There is one underlining benefit of getting varieties of products for display on your store which is drawing more customers to your page. As a merchant, it will be of significant disadvantage to your business when you're stereotypical about your choice of product selection. It is imperative that you are open-minded and accommodate product of other climes. This doesn't nullify making research on extensive research on the product before putting it up on your page.

Scalability

The conventional model of doing business takes extra commitments at every growing stage of your business; you've to work triple what you did when you started. This is one of the advantage dropshipping holds over the conventional mode of trading, and you can quickly scale up your business without the hurdle of working extra. So who works the extra at your scaling point? That is the primary function of your spoiler; they are saddled with the responsibility of meeting with your customers demand no matter the how extensive it might be. Your shelf will never lack anything new and enjoyable since you will continually restock with new products without the fear of satisfying your client. The primary responsibility of the merchant is marketing the product via your online space, once that is handled it is left for the supplier to deliver the good to the consumer.

Whether you're a startup or well-established merchant you can leverage the growing opportunity of dropshipping without breaking a sweat.

The downturns in dropshipping

We've outlined the positive impacts of using the dropshipping model on

116

business, and it does sound endearing. But does this implies that using this model of trade, doesn't mean there are pitfalls? That it is all a walk in the park. No, is the answer. There are downturns in this model of business, and we will carefully examine them below:

Low operating margin

Some merchants are in the business of selling themselves short in a bid to grow revenue for the company. So, they sell at a meager amount so that they can expand their horizon. Although setting up a business using the dropshipping model is not capital intensive that should not compel you to sell yourself short. As a seller, the position you place yourself with your niche has a parallel effect on how people will view your trade. When you have a good website that is graphically engaging (which you might have spent a lot to setup). This will make you shrug off the thought of selling yourself short. You do not compete with anyone, and the sky is spacious for everyone to soar high. Don't pay attention to those merchants who see selling at a low price, as a gimmick to get customers to patronize your business. Avoid being plunged into a small profit margin when you can easily make twice or more of your profit ROI. When you're reasonable enough with your pattern of pricing, then you will have an excellent operational margin.

The small operational cost of starting dropshipping have led to an influx of retailers in the business making it highly competitive. If your supplier sells to different merchants, then your online store slowly loses it value since the goods you have can be seen somewhere else at a lower price. When you're competing with sellers who have the financial legibility to cut down your cost, then it puts you in a tight corner. It means you will have the same products in your virtual space on another clients store going for a price lower than yours. The implication of this is that you might be compelled to go lower in a bid to keep your customers.

The issue with keeping records of stock

This has been a reoccurring issue with merchants that use the dropshipping model. It is way easier to handle goods that are within your care, and you can easily keep track of things and be lord over your product. But in most cases, merchants get stocks from several warehouses to keep their virtual store filled with various product. And that is where the whole confusion stems from. You can even incur debt with this model since there is no balance in your records of supply and the supplier's record. There are ways by which one can successfully synchronize your records with the suppliers, but in most cases, they don't cooperate with using the technology that enhances the operation of the synchronization. The best approach is to have a level of understanding with your supplier on how you can maintain a balanced record on either side.

Merchants are limited in the decision-making process of the goods and solely depends on the supplier's judgment which in most cases might not be in their best interest. You will tell the customer that their products will be available soon and you will be pleading with the supplier to meet your customer need. This put you in an awkward situation with your customer with nobody coming to your aid. In the long run, you will be spending so much in keeping tabs with both the supplier and the customer.

Hike in Shipping charges

This has been an unavoidable problem, merchant face regularly. Why is this unavoidable? Dropshipping helps you get your online space filled up with a wide range of products, all of which might be coming from different suppliers. The suppliers will charge for shipping the products to their location, and it sometimes depends on the type of commodity, it might be lower or sometimes higher. What we're trying to establish is the fact that, you might have to order three different products from different suppliers for a single client which will incur more charges on supplying. This is where the problems lie for most merchants using the dropshipping model of trading. When you sum things up, and it becomes evident that the odds are against you, then you ponder on increasing the cost of the product to cater for the shipping charges. You will only stir up more chaos with that approach because your customers will think they're been extorted and some might go as far as asking for a refund. Making decisions about the shipping charges is a delicate decision especially for a business that uses the drop shipping approach for their business.

119

Suppliers ineptitude

There are times when we find ourselves in situations where we have to take a fall for another person wrongdoing. In some cases, this might be unavoidable especially when you're functioning as de shippers in a business. Suppliers vary regarding attitudes shown towards services, and they capitalize on the fact that you cannot validate the quality of the product to deliver a mediocre product to the client. You will have to take a fall for this because the customer deals with you directly and it is just right to hold you responsible if they're not getting what they want. Although, everybody is susceptible to errors that don't remove the fact that some suppliers are negligent in discharging their services. These poor services can come in a variety of ways from poor packing, missing items, damaged products whatever the customer lost. And customers can easily tag you as being unprofessional with your niche. It is logical you get blamed for your supplier's inefficiency and unprofessionalism in service delivery. The customers know you, and they're most likely oblivious of the existence of a third party supplier. In a situation such as this, you are left with no other option than to refund all that the customer has lost concerning time and monetary value. You will do this in a bid to secure your reputation and business and possibly bid your customer goodbye if they're not willing to patronize you another.

Nobody ever said using dropshipping is going to be a walk in the park, there are pitfalls and if you're not the resilience type you might lose interest in trading after a short period. All these challenges can be overcome when you place yourself in a more advantageous position. You can achieve this when you carefully plan and outline your transaction and work closely with it. This article also describes advantages that comes with drop shipping an what you stand to benefit as a drop shipper. Some people are of the opinion that one of the top benefits drop shipping is that it is not capital intensive. You can find office space in your home and start making good earnings. All you need is a suitable website and a good internet connection.

Chapter 14:
How to Trademark your Business Name

You know what a trademark is, but what you may not know is how it operates; you are not alone in this as many business people who have no business with TM may not understand how it works. The good news for you is that Trademark is for everyone who has a company to protect; it is a business permit granted to prevent the duplicity of a business name by the competition. For a proper understanding of what a trademark is and how it works, this guide will revolve around a story; a favorite story I must say.

A trademark story
In 2012, Beyonce and Jay-z had their baby and named her Blue Ivy. They had a unique business idea for the baby and decided to file a trademark to protect the idea. Thus the name Blue Ivy Carter was filed as a trademark. The purpose was to trademark the name for a baby line products business. The trademark was granted because the name is unique and there is no one with similar trademark in baby products line of business.

What is a trademark?
It is a sign, a symbol that can represent and distinguish a product or service from other products and services; it may consist of words, such as personal or business name, figurative elements, and letters, numbers designed by the trademark owner to represent a product or

service.

Features of a trademark

It is for a business purpose;

It must be unique and not in any way related or like any other name, symbol or shape;

The name must be original to the owner and should not be mistaken for another name.

The same name can be granted in business, not in the same niche or industry

Understanding Trademark Name Restrictions

Trademarks convey an exclusive right to words, phrases, symbols, or designs to name a business. It can be used in ecommerce to represent the company. Therefore, you can trademark a business name, not a name intended for personal use.

It would interest you to note that Blue Ivy granted to Beyoncé's by the USPTO was for a business purpose not for the sole use of her child. That is why a similar name was issued to another applicant using Blue Ivy as a wedding planner!

Reasons to refuse trademark name:

Suggestive names that give an impression without mentioning the actual name will not pass trademark approval such as 'Easy-Off' for an oven cleaner!

Names of common usage such as water, rain, sun, moon,

Jesus, God cannot pass as a trademark;
Names likely to confuse with another trademark will not pass patency scrutiny.

Trademark a name

Anyone one with business intention can trademark a name that meets the criteria for a trademark. You don't have to be big or small in business, as long as you have a big business idea and you want a name protected for it, you can follow the steps below for trademark!

Step #1: Trademark Search

This exercise helps to establish if the name you intend filling for the trademark is available or not. The process involves querying USPTO database if a similar name exists either as pending or registered. Also, if the name is not currently being registered or registered, the search also provide information on whether the name is fit for registration or not; if it contravenes any provision of trademark registration, the search will indicate so and warn of possible rejection when filed for registration.

Further search, more comprehensive finding would search state trademark database, directories and online to ascertain if it's available or not and if you can proceed with your application.

Step #2: File a trademark registration application

After the search and the result indicate you can proceed, the next step is to approach USPTO with an application filed on their online trademark application portal. The application detail will include the following:

> The mark's owner's name and address;
>
> The name being filed for trademark protection;
>
> The intended use of the name (goods or services) to register;
>
> The basis for applying: either use in commerce (if the name is already in use) or for the intended purpose (if it's not in use yet);
>
> If your filing is for use in commerce, a specimen such as a label or a package that shows your name in use; if filing on intent to use, you will provide sample later;
>
> Pay trademark filing fee of $225-325 per class of products or services as of 2016.

Step #3: Respond to Office Actions and Oppositions

> Office Action letter. USPTO attorney will review your application; if there is an issue, the office will write a letter called Office Action to explain the problem and allow you specified time to respond. Do ensure to respond within the stipulated time frame.
>
> Official Gazette. After the review, the application is published in official gazette for public awareness and possible objections. If there is any opposition, you may need the assistance of an attorney for resolution.
>
> Registration/Notice of Allowance. After official gazette and all issues resolved, the trademark is registered if the business is active and in use; for registration by intent, a Notice of Allowance is issued granting the use of the trademark, but the name will not yet be registered until the business intended has

taken off!

After you complete a trademark registration, you are allowed to start using the name with the symbol, ®, coming next to the name. At this point, you can file a lawsuit against anyone who infringes on your trademark, so be on the watch!

Chapter 15:
Apply for LLC for your Online Business

On the road to building a successful digital business, you need to think the legality of your ecommerce because notwithstanding working online; your success may be hindered if your legitimacy is in question.

Mostly, more than anything else, every ecommerce needs to settle their legal identity to win the trust of customers. Therefore, this chapter will discuss how to incorporate an ecommerce to become a legal entity the customers can trust anywhere in the world.

1. What is business incorporation?
2. Types of business legal structure
3. How to incorporate an ecommerce
4. Frequently Asked Questions about incorporating an ecommerce

1.   What is business incorporation?

It is important to note that business incorporation applies to all forms of businesses whether brick and mortar or ecommerce. You should know that every online business has a country of residence; and for such business to be deemed legal, it needs to incorporate with the legal authority in-charge of registering a business in that country.

Therefore, business incorporation is the stipulated legal process of creating a new business or formalizing the legality of an existing business to be recognized as an entity under the presiding law of the business country of domicile and certified as a legal entity.

Depending on the type of business legal structure, the business after incorporation can be treated as a distinct entity from its founder that can sue and be sued under the law.

2.   Types of business legal structure

In the US there are six types of business structures; these include Sole Proprietorship, Limited Liability Company (LLC), Partnership, Cooperative, Corporation, and S-Corporation.

Sole Proprietorship

This is not per se an incorporated business; it is a business registration arrangement to formally register the business as a legal entity recognized by law. The form and structure of the business are the same as the owner.

This type of business registration is better for an individual wanting to start out in ecommerce without the full legal requirements for other forms of business structure. A sole proprietorship has a similar identity with the owner and not required to file a separate tax return.

Limited Liability Company – LLC

LLC is a hybrid business having the features of sole proprietorship and corporation liability protection. This form of business structure differs from state to state and like sole proprietorship is not required to file a tax return but pay taxes on the LLC's profit directly.

While the business has to pay profit tax, its members need to file separate income tax as well. The process of forming an LLC is more demanding than sole proprietorship; it requires an attorney or certified accountant to register an LLC.

Partnership
It's a business structure involving two owners who own the business according to a standing agreement between the two people. A partnership can be general, where the business is evenly divided between the partners; it can also be a limited partnership where there is a limit of both control and liability for specific partners.
Registering a partnership is easier, much like the sole proprietorship, but registration requirements differ from state to state.

Cooperative
Registering as a cooperative for ecommerce can be unusual but not impossible. This form of business serves the interest of members; essentially, cooperative customers are its own members. It is common to have a labor union becoming a cooperative, helps its members online.

Corporation
This form of business structure is a legal entity different from the owners; the owners cannot be sued for the business problems. The regulation for starting a corporation differs from state to state; however, registering a corporation requires the need to register a company first.

129

A corporation pays federal tax and must comply with full details of tax laws at the local, state and federal levels of tax administration. A corporation is required to have a tax-id and abide by business rules for its industry.

S-Corporation
S-Corporations are Regular Corporation who qualified to be on the list of S-Corporation companies as set up by the US internal revenue service (IRS) to prevent double taxation for such companies. These companies pay tax just once and are so immune for multiple taxes.

S-Corporation companies follow similar record keeping assignments of a corporation which require dedicated financial and managerial administration to sort out.

3.   How to incorporate an ecommerce
Before incorporating your business, you need to determine which business structure is best for you. As an online business entity, it is advisable to start as a sole proprietorship which gives you the latitude to manage your business with recognition of the business law in your country and without the burden of a corporation.

To register your online business in the US, or your country of residence, you will need to research the local business registration law as applied to you and follow the process of getting registered as a legal entity.

For this discussion, we will discuss how to incorporate a business in the US:

Each state in the US has a different registration process to incorporate your business; you can visit the USA.gov small business website to access relevant business services. It is pertinent to visit State and Territory Business Resources page on the site to incorporate your business.

If you are not in the US, you can search for relevant government authority handling business registration; preferably, talk to an attorney or certified accountant how to incorporate a business in your environment.

Good luck!

4. Frequently Asked Questions about incorporating an ecommerce

4.1   In which state should I incorporate my online business?

You need the same business incorporation for both ecommerce and brick and mortar business, and it is advisable to incorporate in the state where you intend to conduct your business. However, if you find a state with more business accommodating policies, nothing is stopping you from incorporating your business in that state.

4.2   What is a business license and is it necessary to operate my Internet business?
A business license is a business tax certificate issued by the state where you operate, and it is a mandatory document to register your business. Therefore, you need a business license to register your business correctly. You may also need a wholesale or retail business license and a Federal Tax-ID according to the type of business you do. Note also that business license is different according to state.

4.3   Can I buy and own domain names as a business entity?
Absolutely! It's advisable to buy and own domain names for your ecommerce because it's the virtual address of your online business location and a good plan for business expansion. If you buy ahead, it helps you retain unique names for your business for future use. You can do a DBA filling to use such domains under fictitious name filing as provided for by the law; this law, however, differs from state to state.

4.4   Which states will I have to pay sales tax as an online business?
An ecommerce is required to collect and pay a sales tax whenever they deliver a product. However, the law differs from the state it is better to confirm the right position of things from an accountant or tax expert for updated information.

4.5   I operate multiple ecommerce, should I file a series of LLC?
The series LLC originated in Delaware, but some other states laws, like

Illinois and Oklahoma, also provide for a series LLC. It is like an organizational umbrella of one LLC with multiple "cells." They are generally of interest to individuals with several large assets.

The benefit is the asset protection and anonymity provided to its members, and cost savings recognized through the reduction of paperwork compared with organizing separate LLCs for every business. When properly formed and maintained it would treat each cell as a separate entity, having its own rights and obligations. It means if someone filed a suit against a single series and won, only the assets of that cell is at risk.

Chapter 16:
Branding

Understanding branding and everything that goes with it

The wish of every entrepreneur is for their business to become household name be the choice of every buyer in their niche. However, desires alone don't do the magic of branding; only knowledge and action can help you to achieve what you sincerely hope to get.

In this chapter, we will discuss branding in a layman understanding so you can know what it is and what is involved in building a brand that works for your business. In this chapter, we will discuss the following:

1. What is branding?
2. How can I define my brand?
3. What are brand expectations?
4. Where does design come into branding?
5. How does branding design work?
6. What are some of the most famous brands in the world and why are they so famous?
7. How can I get my business branding right?

So let's take a leap into the amazing world of branding, and take a look.

1.　What is branding?

To understand branding, you need to know what a brand is. The mistake many are making about branding is to think about logo anytime they hear the word brand; brand refers to the idea or image of a product or business that consumers connect with, they identify the name, the logo, slogan, color, and design of the company that owns the idea or image.

Therefore, branding is the processes that deliver your brand to your target audience. How your target market and indeed anyone in such market perceives your business, product, and company when they hear the name or see your logo. That is the first and immediate impression people have about your company is determined by branding.

Branding involves a series of activities that shape the perspective of your audience about your company according to how you want them to think, say and see your business and product. It is a way a company builds its reputation and company assets identification and raise people's genuine expectation and delivers quality service promises to the target audience.

You can define branding as a marketing activity to create a name, symbol that your target audience can quickly be identified as belonging to the company.

Why is branding important?

Branding is important because it creates a memorable impression on consumers and allows the target audience to know what to expect from the company and do the following:

- Helps to get recognition
- Increases business value
- Generates new customers
- Improves pride and satisfaction
- Creates trust within the marketplace

Branding processes

Branding processes go through 6 stages of brand creation:

- Business goals and brand personality
- Market and user research
- Logo design
- Visual elements of a brand
- Corporate brand style
- A style guide

2.   How can I define my brand?

A brand is more than logo design; its more about how to connect your audience with your company on multi-channels through different brand touch points. Your job is to define your brand to describe as an entity with its own voice, and personality; to differentiate your brand, you need to determine what identifies your brand, it is called brand identity.

If you want to define your brand, you need a brand strategy to deliver quality brand accurately; to do this, answering the following questions would form the basis of your brand strategy:

- What are some of their core values?
- What do they stand for?
- What makes their product unique?
- What is their unique selling point?
- Who are their target customers?

By answering and knitting together, the above questions would bring clarity to your brand and help you to define and establish quality and lasting brand your target market will connect with at all times.

Defining your brand may need the help of professional branding agency who has the knowledge to guide you to provide the right information towards building a sustainable brand. Consider hiring a branding agency to deliver quality brand definition and make your brand for you!

3.   What are brand expectations?

Branding encompasses the promise made by a brand owner to its customers about what to expect when they use its products and services. Not only that, branding tells the audience the attitude, and character of the brand to expect – exceptional customer service, clean business environment, quality products, and excellent after-sales service. The brand expectation is contained in the promise as reeled out in various marketing information to assure the public of excellent brand.

Your brand is consumed because of the direct interactions you had with prospective customers. Everyone who believes your promise expects you to deliver on that promise.

Therefore, the brand expectation is a branding activity that gives direction to your brand and gives your audience a sense of expectations from your brand. It is a brand expectation that drives customers loyalty and sense of belonging to stick with your brand because of what they believe they will get.

Consumers are not interested in what you do; they are interested in how what you do can help solve their problems. This means the expectation a consumer has for your brand is to derive satisfaction from consuming your product and find a solution to their problem.

Building brand expectations
You can build your brand expectations by first understanding the customers you want to serve and create your experience of the solution you propose. To build brand expectations, you need to understand your ideal customers, know what they want, their pains and what will make them happy. It is the result of these activities that will culminate into a brand promise to deliver to your audience and back it up with quality branding to so everyone can resonate with your brand promise.

4.   Where does design come into branding?

Every branding efforts need a professional designer to bring all your brand message to live. Do not make the mistake of thinking a graphic designer is a brand expert; these are two different professions, but they work together to give your brand a face, identity and something people can see and resonate with after all the branding groundwork is complete and ready to go public.

We well-defined brand need a logo, color, slogan, theme and other elements to help the brand owner present it to the target audience. These elements, standing alone, are not your brand; your brand is what makes you unique and stand apart from the competition.

The brand design comes into branding after your brand elements have all be identified and you are ready to start the process of brand creation.

Design helps to visually communicate brand message to the audience and create the expected visual effects to draw attention and give reality to the brand; it creates visuals consistent with the brand.

5.   How does branding design work?

Branding design creates a distinct and cohesive message that ties a brands values, signage, business documents, uniforms, and souvenirs; its overall job is reflected in the following:
- Visual identity, including logos
- Corporate identity (business image)

- Products
- Websites
- Packaging
- Physical environments, for example, shops and offices
- Social media.

Done correctly, branding design creates a brand identity that resonates with the brand's target audience and differentiates it from competitors.

Brand identity design has three components:
- Brand culture and values;
- Brand market positioning;
- Visual brand components.

Steps to create brand identity design
- Define Your Target Customer
- Clarify Your Value Proposition
- Choose Your Brand Colors
- Design Your Logo
- Select Your Brand's Fonts
- Create a Brand Style Guide

The job of branding design is not only about producing the visuals; it is also about creating a brand that is easy for the customer to understand. Thus, branding design is about simplifying the brand message to resonate with the target audience without needing additional explanation.

6.   What are some of the most famous brands in the world and why are they so famous?

The Red Cross

The Red Cross brand is synonymous with medical assistance in time of trouble. It is famous worldwide as a symbol of help in a life and death situation. The brand is at the center of providing a solution to human need when all hope seems lost.

The Red Cross is known and famous for service to humanity and delivers on that brand expectation.

Apple

You are probably reading this content via one of the quality products of Apple, one may ask what has an apple fruit got to do with a highly diversified company, but as we know, your logo carries the definition you gave to it. Apple products are known worldwide, and they deliver on their brand promise.

Ralph Lauren

This brand is known for its global leadership in the design, marketing and distribution of premium lifestyle products, its brand identity is known worldwide because it delivers on its brand promise and meets customers' expectations; think of Ralph Lauren, you will think apparels and lifestyle!

141

Adidas

Adidas exceptional role in world Olympic Games and brand signature for athletes' kits brings this brand to leverage on the following of global sports enthusiasts. The key thing in branding is customer identification and meeting your brand promise of quality.

Google

Google brand is known worldwide because of the role it plays in peoples' lives. Even those without business with Google have been seen to refer to Google when discussing finding useful information on the internet. The search engine giant seems to be the only search provider!

7.   How can I get my business branding right?

Getting your branding right is a matter of your commitment to do it right. Considering the number of works involved in creating a quality brand, you need to consider hiring a professional for your branding needs. Of course, you have a choice between hiring a design agency if you can successfully deliver the core branding services for your brand and allow the graphic designer to produce your visual identity or you hire a branding professional to take over the complete task.

Imagine a homeowner without professional DIY skill in plumbing that wants his plumbing fixed. If you are this person, would you do it yourself to hire a professional plumber?

A brand expert is not a logo creator or graphic designer; he is someone a professional trained in all aspects of branding who knows what to look for and how to help you bring together the different components to build a reliable and successful brand.

Your brand is the soul and life of your business; it is what people see in your business to want to buy from you. Whatever business you do, even if your job is paid warfighter, as far as you need a customer, you need branding to do the selling for you!

Chapter 17:

How to Build a Successful E-commerce Brand

The future of ecommerce is looking good, but it's at its infancy; if you are not leveraging this emerging international business opportunity already, you need to start now.

A study shows that 40% of internet users worldwide have purchased products from the ecommerce store. The world consumers are relying on online businesses to meet their needs. Whether you are targeting B2B or B2C clientele, there are enormous business opportunities for everyone to get a slice of the pie.

According to a Forrester Research, 2016, commerce platforms using online sales will rise at an average of 9.32% yearly for the next 5 years, and consumers online-spending I the United States will hit $523 billion by 2020. It further projected the number of consumers browsing and buying from ecommerce stores on mobile devices to reach 270 million.

More interesting about ecommerce global business opportunity is the fact that we are fast gone past the era of the business barrier and truly living in a global village setting where both small and large business can compete favorably according to their business positioning.

As ecommerce remains promising to change the global economy, there are online business resources to jump start any business to compete with big brands overnight. What today's entrepreneurs need, however, is information and the knowledge to implement relevant business tools to take your ecommerce to the next level.

The following discussion will take us through different topics to build a successful ecommerce brand.
1. What is ecommerce?
2. Options for starting an ecommerce business
3. Exercise
4. Essential ingredients of every successful brand
5. Basics of kick-starting your ecommerce

1.   What is ecommerce?
It is also known as electronic commerce or internet commerce; ecommerce refers to buying and selling of goods and services on the internet involving customer information and financial transactions.

Ecommerce can be understood, simply, as imitating traditional commerce online and eliminating the physical location barrier and other local business laws to transact business online.

Ecommerce can be of different types, the same way there are different types of business in brick and mortar mode of doing business; they include Business to Consumer (B2C), Business to Business (B2B), Consumer to Consumer (C2C), Consumer to Business (C2B).

There are also different forms of transactions in ecommerce such as Retail, Wholesale, Dropshipping, Crowdfunding, Subscription, Physical products, Digital products, and Services.

What is essential about ecommerce is the level of freedom and innovation each player can bring into their business to define the new business edge and market positioning.

2.   Options for starting an ecommerce business

There are various options for an entrepreneur to launch out in ecommerce depending on your level of information, knowledge, resources, and strategy.

To settle for an option, you need to understand the different types of ecommerce and choose your form of transaction to begin your ecommerce journey.

Here are some options you have to start in ecommerce:
• Join existing ecommerce store

You can become a seller on existing ecommerce sites like Amazon, eBay, Shopify, Aliexpress and many more to sell products made by yourself of from other producers.

Thousands of other sellers use these ecommerce platforms in the same niche as you do, and this brings lots of competition, but also brings opportunities to differentiate yourself from the crowd and catch in big on the gains of your marketing innovation.

While joining exiting ecommerce platform can be a quick way to launch yourself into the world of ecommerce, there is a limit to how much you can make compared to when you start your own website and offer yourself to the global market. However, this option has its challenges as well.

Other online platforms to build quick online presence include – Instagram, Facebook, Google, YouTube, LinkedIn, and Pinterest. Use of these platforms requires being innovative to solve other business resources which the real ecommerce stores, like Amazon, provide.

• Join freelancing/job sites
For individual professionals who want to leverage ecommerce to sell their skills, joining freelancing sites help them to set up gigs and offer their services for sale to prospective clients, mostly on a B2B basis.

A freelancing site is similar to ecommerce stores where professional services providers open an account to collect job, process and deliver it in exchange for payment. Skilled individuals can join job sites like Fiverr, Upwork, and Freelancer, etc. to create gigs for sales.

• Build your independent online business
If you have the knowledge and resources, building your own website can make a lot of difference than being on Amazon or eBay. This

process needs having your own website, payment, and marketing systems.

While the retailers on Amazon and Freelancers on Fiverr can decide to continue using the third-party platforms to offer their services, they also have the option to start a website, promote it and attract customers to survive in the world of ecommerce!

Tips to build ecommerce store that makes over $1 million annual income

Position yourself before the right target audience. Truth be told, you need to attract customers to sell your product or service; while this may look so simple to do, the truth is, many businesses have failed in their regards. If you can't get people to buy your product, succeeding online is tough!

Create a unique selling proposition to attract real fans. It is one thing to stand before your target audience and show them what you have; it is another thing to be heard and followed. The only way a customer would listen to you and buy your product or service is if you sell your customers solution to their problem; your USP should convey that solution unambiguously!

Sell solution that works o your audience. Ecommerce sellers that offer a solution that works and find a way to communicate it to the prospective audience will always be in business; buyers want products that work!

3.   Exercise

Decide your unique offer for your consumers and craft a compelling brand story that improves the customer experience.

To do this exercise, do the following:

> You know what you are offering, take time to write a compelling message to tell your audience about the product
> Review the message and make sure it appeals to their emotions and deliver a clear message of your solution
> Review your buyer persona and make sure the message you are writing talks to them
> Let your message position you as the solution provider they need

This exercise has been used by major brands to take their businesses upward of over a million dollars in sales!

The simple advice for you is - "walk the talk."

4.   Essential ingredients of every successful brand

•   Ensure brand Consistency. Ecommerce thrives on trust! One thing that can ruin your brand is inconsistency because it does not convey the confidence or show your audience that you know what you are doing.

Your ecommerce must show consistency in everything that represents you; that means your brand element should not show you as inconsistent because it will send the wrong signal to your prospective customers.

Your messages should show agreement, don't let your logo betray your brand design, color, and your business culture should be in harmony with everything else that represents your brand.

• Ensure quality customer experience. You may not be strong enough to compete with the big guys in ecommerce in term of price, but you can compensate for that by offering a quality user experience that makes your customers feel special. You can achieve this by personalizing your products to your individual customer's need. Adding such experience makes your customers feel special and loved and would surrender their loyalty without asking.

5.   Basics of kick-starting your ecommerce

We have discussed strategies and shared some information to build a successful ecommerce; it's time to get your business off the ground.

• Start with Facebook ads. If you are in a niche business, it's certain your audiences are on the social media giant, Facebook; the best way to meet them is to advertise your ecommerce on the platform. It would be helpful if you learn how to drive sales through Facebook for ecommerce.

• Try Instagram. Facebook gives you the connection to jumpstart your other social media like Instagram where you can visually present your offer for more following. Note that users on visual SM expect high-quality visuals; they will stay with you if you don't disappoint their expectations.

• Experiment with buy button ads. Social media platforms are places to sell your product if you add a buy button to your ads; I suggest you experiment with this, practicing native commerce, to see the outcome.

• Get product influencers. Part of ways to take off with your ecommerce is to have respectable social icons to drive your marketing for you. Product influencers would give you the springboard to bounce on and be seen by their audience who trust their judgment to try out your product.

Ecommerce is the trending global business that can give you a quick launch and stability to build a stable income within a short time. It takes deciding to make it work as there are tons of new things to learn every day.

However, don't be scared by the learning curve involved in ecommerce brand building; there is always someone waiting to handle the task on outsourc

Chapter 18:
Professional Logo Design Process

No brand design work is complete without the inclusion of the logo element to give visual appeal to wrap up the branding activities. You don't want just any logo for your brand, because good logos convey the core beliefs of your business including what you do and your cultural values. As a result, you need a professional logo design to have the best logo design for your brand.

The article discusses logo design where we look at the step-by-step process to have a professional logo for your branding. We understand that each logo design project differs in scope, style, and industry, but they all follow a consistent design process.

Part 1: Initial Graphic Design Process Steps
1   Construct the Creative Design Brief
2   Research & Discovery Phase

Part 2: The Client's Logo Design Process Steps
3   Logo Sketches & Brainstorming
4   Conceptualization
5   Refinement and Client Presentation
6   Feedback and consultation
7   Concept development
8   Completed graphic design presentation

Part 3: The Branding Process Steps
9   Expansion to brand collateral
10   Final files, delivery, and support

10 Steps for Branding Clients

Successful logo design for the brand is about understanding a client's needs; develop the concepts and expanding the plan to meet all forms of clients needs. This ten-step approach to professional logo design is divided into three parts of clearly defined processes.

Part 1: Initial Graphic Design Process Steps

This part contains sections and sub-sections to discuss the design process.

1. Construct the Creative Design Brief

The creative design brief is the first step in every professional logo design. This step is crucial as it helps a designer to understand the client and what they need. Here, the designer must ask questions to have a clear idea of the job, the business, the industry, and the client's concern. This process may be held over the phone, in-person or through an email or chat.

1. What is creative design brief?

It's a document created during a design consultation meeting with the client that contains discussions between the designer and client on the type of logo and the purpose it is needed. Such a meeting is usually a question and answers session where the designer asks predefined questions that will help him design the right logo for the client. As a client, the more clearly you are in answering such problems, the better your logo design outcome.

2. What Questions do professional designers ask Clients? There are no standard questions to ask, but each professional develops unique questions to ask that would help them deliver perfect logo design for their clients. However, these questions will address the following areas of the client's need: About your business, About your customers, and About the project.

2. Research & Discovery Phase
After the professional designer has been briefed about the client's job and needs, he will go over the brief documents to extract vital information to start his work. At this point, he begins by conducting in-depth research to discover how to approach the design assignment.

1. Client discovery
If this is an existing business, the designer looks into their current branding stage to learn about their branding efforts. The reason this is to learn more facts that the client didn't mention in brief to help the graphic designer come up with the best design solution.

2. Industry discovery
It is essential to know the various industries the client's business serves; this helps to know about more competition than the clients has ever

imagined. Industry discovery for a designer helps to emphasize what works and drop what don't.

3. Primary, qualitative and quantitative research

The designer goes deeper to research brand questions for a comprehensive brand identity design solution. This process takes brand questions through qualitative and quantitative research methods to discover more branding issues to address.

This sort of research helps to identify many brand challenges, collect brand data and address target audience attitudinal problems to branding.

The entrepreneur should note that this process is only done in case of professional logo design where the right price is involved; no cheap logo design job will go through this process because it's time-consuming.

4. Secondary research

Where it is necessary, the designer would research further into clients current brand identity to see their existing brand collateral like reports, stationery, and their website. Of course, this reveals more information the client couldn't have included in the initial brief about the logo design.

Part 2: The Client's Logo Design Process Steps

This part contains sections and sub-sections to discuss the design process.

Part 3: Logo Sketches & Brainstorming

In designing a great logo, every design must start with a sketch; irrespective of the final presentation of a logo, the place to start is on paper, to sketch it out to give the idea shape and visual to behold.

1. Mood boards and reference imagery

From the start, mood boards and reference imagery are collected; sometimes this will come from the client that sent over images that portray the look or feel of what they want communicating in the logo design.

Describing 'themes' or colors in words can be difficult, so it's best the client send some visual inspiration if they can.

2. Quick sketches & basic forms

From the first sketch, there could be appealing visual iconography or shapes and worthy of development. Such a stage could take the designer to move to grid paper or dotted paper to redraw and enlarge the original design, and refining with a pen for the next design step.

3. Refining the logo with gridlines

Additional development of the logo sketches could take the form of grids and lines drawn to balance and align things correctly.

Even original shapes can be enhanced with a constructed grid, be it how the logo mark could potentially sit alongside the logotype.

4. Conceptualization

This stage in the design work has gone past the forming of concept stage as you may want to reason by the term, but this is a stage in the process for refining the idea further on a computer, no longer on the paper.

Having the idea of a computer gives it a new viewpoint and allows the designer to observe immediate concerns not seen or overlooked in the sketch.

1. Creating digital versions from the sketchbook

The primary forms are digitally constructed working either with a scanner or recreating manually in Adobe Illustrator. Having the digital versions of the design allows for quick amendments, adjustments and offers the ability to fine-tune the designs accordingly efficiently.

2. Exploration in a monotone

Before applying colors to any design, consideration of the logo must be taken in monotone black and white shades. Black and white are the extremes of color, light, and tone.

There are many poorly created logo designs where the designer did not worry about how the logo would look in black and white. Despite 'fax' dying out, a great logo design should look good in any format, and in any output.

3. Creating a logotype

With some rough ideas to work with for the logo mark, it's time to consider how the company name will be represented through the logotype.

From initial research and discovery activities, the logo designer has a general idea of the style of typeface for the logo, such as a contemporary sans-serif or old style serif, however, finding the perfect font for the job at hand takes browsing through an extensive font library already in place.

Sometimes, where the clients wanted something unique and paid for it, the designer can resort to a customized font to fit the needs of the project. The customized font is advantageous, because it creates a unique quality to the Brand, however, expanding this out to a bespoke typeface may add to the costs involved.

4. Pulling it all together

With a handful of typefaces appropriate to the Brand, the designer will look at how they look side-by-side with the logomark symbols created earlier. Several selected color palettes will be integrated into the design, to see what feels like the strongest approach.

This part of the design process involves many comparison prints to be considered on one-page view.

5. <u>Refinement and Client Presentation</u>

At this stage, the strongest logo concepts are collated into a client presentation document to show how the logo looks on different background colors, at different scales, and alongside some logo mockups. This is to help the client visualize their logo in reality, rather than just central on a page.

1. Color Scheme Exploration

The client now has the benefits of seeing alternative color schemes to help visualize the potential of the concept.

Since color is very subjective, and a simple shift of hue can make the world of difference, this stage helps the client see different color variations to help the client make the right choice.

2. Future-proofing adaptability

Reflection of 'how' the logo may look in future is taken; a professional logo needs to be timeless, to prevent issues down the line, or appear out of date in just a few years.

3. Creating digital mockups

Digital mockups show how a concept could look in real life if the client were to use it on a shirt; this process can help the client see the idea itself over the visual aesthetic.

The Professional designer spends some time to create appropriate mockups to give the client the right feel of an impression how the logo will stand out when used on an object such as T-shirt, cup, cap or vehicle!

4. Logo design presentation o client

The initial logo design presentation is outputted in a secure PDF format, to allow the client to view it on screen or print out.

Where the fund is available, it is recommended to print to see the live presentation and correct any concern such as color not showing accurately. Each concept has its PDF, comprising 5–10+ pages depending on the project scope.

6. Feedback and consultation

Clients are advice to spend a few days, or a week, with the initial concepts, although first impressions are always worth noting. You can print them out, stick them around where you can see it – house or office to let eyes be drawn to them randomly, and naturally, in a real-life situation of encountering the Brand.

Get feedback from trusted people - friends and family, and current employees who understand the Brand because they are stakeholders.

Even, with mixed opinions, all are valid and provide direction that allows the designer to improve any issue that came up.

Next stage is a meeting or feedback provided via email asking the designer press forward; sometimes, the designer may have more questions to extract detailed feedback from the client further.

1. Discuss logo concept with the client

Sometimes, the designer would discuss the ideas with the client to gauge feedback. This may be a brief discussion if the client has found one of the concepts to be perfect; it could also be lengthy discuss if they found any uncertainties that need clarifying. This process is integral to a professional graphic design process!

2. Advise and provide guidance on selection

Usually, when a designer presents initial concepts to the client, he would have a view on the 'strongest' idea from the beginning and showing the client these inherent qualities is often part of the talk.

3. Discuss potential developments the client would like to see

Developments differ significantly between projects, but in general, it is easier to develop the artistic side compared to the conceptual.

Aspects such as an alternate color scheme or typeface can change the 'look,' but the significance or meaning behind a logo is not as easy to modify.

7. Concept development

According to the feedback and discussion with the client, the designer would look into developing and tweaking the preferred concept. This could be minor changes to the color scheme by looking at different layouts or presenting alternative typefaces for consideration.

In nearly every case, one concept would be perfect for the client, while in a few instances, more time may be spent where the client finds it hard to decide.

Customarily, at this stage, only one or two development cycles are needed, as it comes down to a color or style element.

8. Completed graphic design presentation

This stage involves a more focused approach, like the initial concepts presentation, where one concept has been fully fleshed out. Further mockups, and realized business cards or stationery could be presented as the next logical step.

Part 3: The Branding Process Steps

This part contains sections and sub-sections to discuss the design process.

9. Expansion to brand collateral

After signing off the final logo design, providing that is not the end of the project based on the client's needs, the designer can move to expand the logo onto the further branding process steps.

A typical example, in this case, is the company stationery. This will include the creation of everything from company letterhead, business cards, and marketing materials.

1. Create branded stationery based on the final logo design

According to the client's physical location, consideration must be made of the local stationery dimensions. For instance, the UK and US printers see a letterhead differently. A professional graphic designer often has several templates to meet global clients' location needs, so it is a case to build the specific layouts.

2. Expand the branding onto social media elements

Clients need to think about creating their social media design where the approved logo can fit such sections including social network profile images, the banners, and headers; current dimensions are used to ensure everything looks perfect to reveal the new Brand Identity to the world.

3. Provide any Further Brand Collateral Required—Vehicle Wraps, Signage, etc.

This Graphic Design process step is always individual to the client; this is because it's not applicable to every business; not every company needs external signage for instance, especially in ecommerce.

Businesses with brick and mortar model, like a gym, would need to be branded uniforms, salesperson car, salesroom, vehicle wraps, and signage. If your business doesn't need any of these, you don't have to bother yourself.

10. <u>Final files, delivery, and support</u>

The logo design is done in Adobe Illustrator, in vector form exportable in any format required.

The standard files will consist of: (.AI, EPS/.PDF, .JPEG and.PNG)
The Vector file allows for the maximum range of output because you can scale the size without the logo losing its quality or sharpness.

Mostly, you have a logo you can use across the board for your business, no matter the application, including a billboard.

1. Export all final files and organize

The final project files are neatly arranged for easy location when the client needs it with all formats and layouts are included, including monotone (black and white) versions for varied backgrounds use.

In case there is any 'layout' design, like brochures or marketing flyers, files will include InDesign package to include the images and fonts used, where applicable.

2. Create brand guidelines document

Brand Guidelines show how the Brand is to be presented to the world.
It can be passed along to a web developer to see the exact color values quickly to be used on the website and know what fonts are to be utilized

for the web content.

Also, the guidelines are useful for the printer to ensure utmost accuracy when the documents are printed, through Pantone color values.

3. Send ZIP to client and archive in Dropbox

The entire design and relevant design information are zipped up and sent in an email to the client, copying additional employees that need access to the original files.

The designer would then archive the ZIP file into our Dropbox, to serve as a backup should the client misplace the designs.

4. Ensure Client understands all Final Files and gives Usage Instructions

The designer wants to make sure the client understands how to use the designs submitted, so they are on hand to assist the client relating to the project at any point in the future.

5. Further notes on the Logo Design Process Steps for Branding Clients

As earlier mentioned, every project is different, and that makes being a branding agency most enjoyable. Thus, not every project will go through all the steps above; not every client will fund every stage as described.

For instance, the client may just need a professional logo design for their startup, which will not be sensible to allocate budget into further Branding.

They may have already done market research in-house, such information can be submitted to the designer, without the need to repeat the process, and move to the next stage.

This Graphic Design process for clients Logos and Branding is useful for entrepreneurs to understand the process involved in designing great branding logos and can as well be useful for a logo designer to help in providing logo design services.

Chapter 19:

Best E-commerce Platforms

Introduction

E-commerce has experienced a great deal of change over the past 2-3years. And for those who want to join this voyage, it is vital they understand what contributed to this development. Although mobile and social media contributed immensely to this development, the world is slowly moving pass that realization. And embracing other new inventions, that is expected to the change the face of e-commerce in the coming years.

With technology such as artificial intelligence, customization, digital wallets and mobile, e-commerce is set to take the world by storm in the coming years and future. People can quickly scroll through the internet and make a purchase of their product of choice with just a single click. For someone to make that decision, they must have found both the page and the product appealing. It is way easier to draw the attention of a potential customer to your page when it catchy and endearing. I mean it possesses everything that will attract the attention of every human.

That's where the use of e-commerce platform comes to play, and it is only through their platform you can easily make your mark as a seller.

We're in a fast-paced world which makes most of our activities where everything seems to move fast. This implies for you to be successful running an e-commerce platform or a business model you must have the required tools at your disposal. Make extensive research on the type of platform that will fit perfectly to needs of your product and also attract the right kind of customer. I've taken the time to study and research on the best e-commerce platforms, and I was able to draw down the list to top seven e-commerce. Whichever, type of business model you operate you will find them beating your expectation and helping you stay prolific in the e-commerce space. This is coming from a realist, e-commerce has been more of a loggerhead these past years and what is apparent is a continuity in this competitiveness. What keeps you on top is if you have the right information at your disposal. Join me as we outline each of this platform:

1.   Shopify

Since its inception into the online trading platform, Shopify has been exemplary through their use of social media and mobile platforms to help meet the needs of their clients. The Canadian-based e-commerce platform have been everyone one-stop solution, breaking grounds with the use of state the art technology. They're moving in line with the fast-paced trend we're witnessing in the e-commerce space. They offer your client a seamless shopping experience, stacking up their virtual cart without leaving their social media page. It doesn't matter how old your enterprise is or if it's been sitting in the mortar and bricks for donkey tears, what matters most to Shopify is giving your product that voice that helps it gets heard. To cap it all, what dignifies Shopify from other e-commerce platform is bringing vendors from different niches such as designers and whatnot. To bring their products to a platform serving as a one-stop shop for all retailers.

Pros:

Shopify allows you to turn your Facebook page to a digital supermarket for just $9. You can do this by merely integrating your Facebook account with your Shopify store.

Cons:

Despite all the benefits outlined above, there are still some downsides with owning a store on Shopify. Most of which comes with paying extra on certain services even after paying to get registered on the platform. Take, for example, if you fail to make use of the Shopify payment then you will be charged extra, and most of the great extension on the platform comes with extra charges. I think for most people what would be the most difficult of all these is getting customization on their page due to the coding language used by Shopify.

The verdict:

Based on consensus, Shopify is the most user-friendly platform at the moment. And that's a good selling point for the platform, helping every newbie who yearns for a traditional system of transactions to make a sale within a short period. Their standard package ranges from $29 to $299, and it also depends on the type of package that you want.

2.   Magento

Since it started operation in 2008, Magento has grown tremendously not just because of its open-source framework but serving as a recliner even to startups businesses. They don't falter in their service delivery, and customers get to enjoy an impressive scalability level on their website. For sellers with a few numbers of product on their shelf, you can multiply your product and start making great outreach with the scalability level of Magento. They also provide cool theme features that help you give your customer an excellent shopping experience. An average seller might get swamped up with so many options due to the variety of options on the page. Most times users need the help of an expert programmer to turn down the robustness of the platform to meet their comprehensiveness level. There are quite a number of popular brands that use this platform, brands such as Liverpool FC, Huawei, Pepe jeans, burger king and a host of others.

Cons:

The major drawback with Magento is that the platform is not meant for anyone that doesn't know to programme. Although, there is a free package moving to the significant enterprise level cost $20,000 per annum. This is not without the extra amount you might need to hire an excellent software programmer if you don't have any working for you or part of your team. All of these are the major drawbacks that are worthy of consideration if you are considering using Magento.

The verdict:

If you're a big brand or you have a big enterprise, then Magento is the perfect outlet for your product, assuming that you have the capital and software programmers to help get you settled. Small and medium scale business might need to look somewhere else asides this platform considering it cost for starting up. Another aspect is the availability of the technical management team since it requires a high level of programming skills which might get you to hire a skillful programmer or possibly pay a third-party freelancer programmer. To help put your site in shape before you can begin to make sales.

3.   **Yokart**

We finally have a space where startups and medium scale business can post their products. A lot of platforms have a multi-vendor version, but yokart is specially developed for this need. No doubt, it is known for offering market solutions to a multi-vendor platform such as Amazon, eBay, Etsy, and so many others. They recently upgraded to yokart 8 which comes with the multilingual and use of other currencies which will

171

help vendors to get customers from different part of the world. It doesn't stop there; it gets even better with it several payment gateways, analytical tools, and discount payment features. If what you desire is satisfying your needs as a multi-vendor then look no further yokart has got you covered. They have tools that are primarily tailored towards fulfilling this needs. Check out their page to see the fantastic shipping calculator that is distinctive for different sellers in various part of the world. The team of developers of this platform is concerned about securing the data of users on the platform, and they do this through the use of the multilayer security system. So that retailers can concern themselves with other essential aspects such as making sales on their products.

Pros:

As a store owner on the platform, once you get access to the source code, you're guaranteed of a lifetime license.

Cons:

When you consider the number of benefits this platform holds, one would have doubted if it has any demerits. It has some downsides, first being that you will need the services of a programmer who is good with PHP to help with customizing your page. It is primarily tailored towards small and medium scale business and it inbuilt features have been categorized according to the package which you like.

The verdict:

It is certain that startups will thrive on this platform. The price for the basic package is very much affordable which if $250, and it comes with a one year license. You can use the basic package to see how well your business will perform in the long run, before going for other higher packages. Once you have tested this out, then you can check other amazing packages such as the Go quick, Gocustome lite, and go custom. Each of these packages is very beneficial, and they all come with success story from customers who are using them.

4.   Bigcommerce

Bigcommerce is a favorite brand who have been providing a timeless solution to the needs of e-commerce platforms, whether they're startups or big brands. Popular brands Martha Stewart and Toyota uses this platform, and it is noted to have well over 55,000 stores subscribed on its platform. They have been helpful to most startups in time past and till present helping them to their product at the forefront of their store. The appealing part is that people with zero coding skills can also make use of the platform, customizing their page and using other critical features on the platform.

Cons:

If what you want is an e-commerce platform that comes with multi-vendor features then Bigcommerce is not the best place for you. You're also liable to get a maximum of seven free themes, which when compared to other platforms where you can get as much as 20 free themes to customize your online store. But that aside, you can utilize its premium features which comes with a whole lot of themes that you can use to customize your page for a fantastic selling experience.

The Verdict:

Bigcommerce removes the laden of learning how to code or searching for a professional that can; you only choose to learn to code if it pleases you not for your online store needs. If you're confident you can leave without themes or make do with the seven free themes on their platform, then you certainly have no problem. You can as well subscribe to their premium theme features.

5.   VTEX

The Brazilian cloud based e-commerce platform raked a whopping sum of $1.6billion on it merchandise platform. They have a host of big brands like Coca-Cola, Walmart, Disney, L'Oreal, and a host of others on their platforms. They are the one-stop platform for local businesses.

Pros:

One of their selling points is the "password-free checkout" feature which in the past year has increased its conversion rate to 54%. It has also contributed to the increase in its revenue and organic traffic which stands at 28% and 30% respectively.

Cons:

What they made us believe is that businesses using the cloud-based e-commerce platform have more likelihood of becoming successful when compared to their traditional e-commerce platform. Their framework is built on the saas network which means you won't have full control over your online store. This has been one major turn off for most small and medium scale business. From the onset, you might have noticed the platform is tailored towards rich brands and the rationale behind that is the cloud-based network it offers which startups might not afford.

The verdict:

Only businesses that are well established that make a turnover of over $1.8million can benefit from the fantastic features of vtex which includes its high conversion rate. Startups might consider pitching their tent somewhere else due to the running cost of starting an online store on the platform.

6.   Woocommerce

Woocommerce has gradually become a household name spreading its tentacles in different parts of the world and merchants are benefiting immensely from it free word press plugin. Not to forget its secure payment and shopping cart feature which makes it more endearing for users. You will have a cutting-edge experience on the platform if you're familiar with the use of WordPress. You can opt your sales activities by going for the multi-vendor version of the platform which requires getting additional WordPress plugin.

Cons:

We all know Woocommerce comes free, but the complete integration of the store with your online store requires paying extra. Noteworthy of mention is the scalability level of this platform which might hold you back once your business starts growing. The platform begins to slow down tremendously once your business starts expanding. And the complete roadblock is that operating Woocommerce requires full knowledge of WordPress. The implication is getting yourself a WordPress expert on your team or learning how to use it.

The verdict:

Woocommerce supports that spirit of complacency, so if you're not concerned about growing your business, then you have no problem working on this platform. Not to forget, finding an expert in Wordpress or taking out time to get yourself use to the platform.

7. Ticktail

Ticktail's mechanism and buildup is based on intuition, and the attention is tailored towards the attractiveness of your page, ease of usage. The platform offers retailers in the fashion industry to show off their fantastic clothing designs to the world, by setting up their account within minutes and begin to make returns on investment.

Cons:

One of the downsides of ticktail is the limited option for payment, not when you see other e-commerce platform making the payment process more accessible for their subscribers. Merchants are required to make payment on every sale made on ticktail, but the custom shop features allow you to sell for free and only charge and affordable on a yearly basis. All of which is happening despite the instruction by the global marketplace that every product sold on ticktail comes with a price.

The verdict:

If you have the intention is taking your business to a different horizon then ticktail is the right e-commerce platform for you. They have got the tools and features that can help startups find their footing in the online marketplace. However, this platform might not cut it for established platforms and big brands.

Conclusion

As individuals, we've different needs, and we find solace to our problems from different outlet depending on what works for you. Now what works for you might not work perfectly or work at all for me, which brings about the law of individualism. This is quite similar to businesses and e-commerce platform; every company has its own distinctive need and an e-commerce platform that can meet that need. So don't get your expectation too high and expect one e-commerce platform to meet all of your business needs. We highlighted seven top e-commerce and discussed vital features that make them beneficial to every business. The demerit mentioned is no indication that the platform is not efficient, but we're trying to guide you in making an informed business decision when you're about getting an e-commerce platform for your business.

Ensure you do extensive research on whichever platform you would like to settle for, choose wisely and watch your business develop at a faster pace.

Chapter 20:
E-commerce shipping plans

Introduction

Every e-commerce platform must have a firm hold on their shipping strategy, and it is one of the critical aspects that help grow your business. Although, some might choose to run free shipping or post an honest USPS rating. For you to be successful in the online market space, you need to be pragmatic and come up with a reasonable shipping plan. This not only creates a mark among your contemporaries but also increases your profit margin. To achieve a good shipping strategy in your organization you need to sensitize every party involved in the process. Getting them on board with your plan on revamping the shipping strategy of your organization and inundated them on individual responsibility in developing the country. This is primarily the only way you can achieve a reasonable profit margin while making your client happy. This write has been tailored towards guides that can help your organization achieve success with it shipping strategy.

The best approach to e-commerce shipping

1. Get the right team onboard: Each section in your company have a role to play towards hashing out the shipping plans of your organization

2. Make your goals apparent: what do you want? Higher profit margin? Make your goal distinctive and walk towards achieving it

3. Select a shipping method: There are primarily four methods of shipping, but free shipping is off the table

4. Take a bold step: the ability of starting is the ability to get ahead.

Let's set the ball rolling.

Getting the right team onboard

Identifying people with like minds who're goal driven within your organization is the first and most significant of all the steps. You need to go through a mental process of what questions you will ask them, to decipher if they're down for this cause. I will share a breakdown of how you can build your thought process towards having likeminded people on your team. This will come in the form of a checklist and will be broken down into four categories.

Marketing

The marketing team are most likely the first point of contact with potential customers, it is significant they get them informed on the shipping options the company offers. They can mention promotional offers like free shipping or the flat rate offer.

Web design and development

The availability of a wealth of information at the proper time is as important as having the information. Your team needs to see how vital it is to have the right information at the right time. Making the information concise and straightforward will make it easier to understand to people visiting your organization website.

Fulfillment

This team is vital towards bringing smiles to the faces of your customers since they will be concerned with the picking, packing, and shipping of your customer's package. They have to work with whatever shipping option the customer demands regardless of what it might take to make that happen.

Customer service

This team needs to be informed of how a poor shipping option can leave a severe scar on customers and might need to put themselves in the shoes of the client to have a first-hand perception of what it feels to get a bad service experience.

Making your goals apparent

After going through the process of identifying and selecting the right people to help develop the shipping strategy of your organization, then it is about time you mention what you plan to actualize with these goals.

There are several goals worthy of consideration under this section, but we will highlight the notable ones:

-Shipping strategy goals for e-commerce platform:
-Rise in conversion rating
-Getting more order value
-Increasing customer base
-A steady drop in cost
-Efficiency in the working mechanism

Rise in conversion rating

When you offer the right kind of delivery options that your customers want, then you're variable contributing to the conversion rate of your business. Try out either of the shipping options you have in stock for your customers and see which of them is most loved through the customer review section on your page.

Getting more order value

You can begin by offering a slash in the price of certain commodities to draw the attention of people and through you will get more orders on your products. People love discounts, and that should be your catching point or run promotional offers.

Increase customer base

You can break new grounds by considering international shipping or other forms of navigation that is not common to people in your location. Reach out to places where people have never had any contact with your product. Collaborate with the marketing team to reach to clients from other parts of the world through social media and other search tools.

A steady drop in cost

Carry out in-depth research on other shipping options from major carriers that can help to bring the price of shipping a reasonable amount. Shipping companies such as UPS and FedEx have packages that can help you keep the cost of shipping to a fair amount. One of such is the FedEx smart post, which comes with excellent service delivery and affordable price.

Efficiency in the working mechanism

The fulfillment team is the final point of contact with the consumer which implies that a proper packaging of the goods will influence the customer's decision to trade with you another time.

Selecting a shipping method

At this stage, you must have gone through the rudiments of finding the right players in your team and getting them on board about what you're playing for. The next point of action is coming up with a shipping strategy that will enhance the process of achieving your goals. We will outline some basic strategy and try to see their benefits and downturns.

Before we move too far, let me bring to your attention that as the project owner of a shipping strategy there are some underlining factors you need to consider.

Vital Shipping Consideration

Results gotten from research, polls, and surveys carried on a yearly basis on e-commerce are uniform, and it indicates that; it is crucial to offer your customer the best shipping rate there is and also laying down other options to foster the growth of your business. However, what appears to be important which is the cost of shipping is the least concern for most customers. What matter most is the shipping options on the ground and the pace at which you deliver the goods. These two conditions will prevent issues such as rejecting products and maximizing sales.

You can take up the management of shipping strategy in your organization and meet the needs of your customers which is a low shipping rate and still maximize sales. Let's take a keen look at three factors worthy of consideration when taking over the shipping section of your business.

Product scale

The size and weight of a product are not much of a concern and in most cases the easiest to understand. If your items are uniform, then you have the option of using a location-based pricing system. For products that are not uniform which happens mostly, you can get feedbacks from significant carriers like DHL, UPS, FedEx and so on. To compare with what you're offering your client and see if it's a good deal. The practical approach to this is breaking your goods into groups based on the heaviest and lowest; you can run a 20% check on the most ponderous and lowest respectively. This is the best way to appropriate your plan so that it has a positive effect on your ROI.

Shipping based on location

This aspect varies significantly; you can only be a judge of this if you're shipping locally. When shipping domestically you can offer discounted prices on shipping, flat rate offer or a free shipping package. The only drawback is when shipping outside the shores of your country, and your best bet is to get the rating from carriers to shape your pricing fee on the product.

Shipping options

The quality of the product you're bringing to your clients is as important as the quality of shipping service. This is one way in which you can see

185

them happy when you make your delivery timely. There are local carriers in major cities around the world that offer prompt delivery service compared to the big shipping company that has so many customers to pick up from. Local carriers provide all of these services at a competitive price, and you should consider using them for your delivery needs. It is vital that you take charge and take cognizance of every detail. There are cases where you don't need local carriers especially for international delivery, say from Washington to Beijing. Ensure that you're getting the value for your money and leave no stone unturned. There will be no rationale behind using a freight service to deliver a shirt, that would be a total waste of resource.

Here are top delivery options e-commerce platform uses.

> -Free shipping
> -LTL freight carriers
> -Same day delivery
> -Free in-store pickup

Free shipping

This is the easiest of them all, and everyone understands it's benefits and loves to jump on it. Amazon started it and placed a tag of $25 upward, and since then it has become a ritual in the e-commerce trade. Let's take a look at the benefits of free shipping to retailers:

- Customers easily grasp the meaning.

- It always beat customers' expectations

- It brings a good conversion rate for customers who made it past their virtual cart.

Offering your customer this type of options means you have to be calculative. At first, you have to set a price tag for customers to get free shipping. Then make sure you're putting it on a product that you're making a substantial profit from.

Flat rate and table rate shipping

This has been the most effective method of dodging the problem that comes with Free Shipping. You will find each of the options interesting.

What does flat rate in e-commerce means?

This implies putting an exact shipping price on every product irrespective of the type of product, and it is instrumental for most retailers. Take, for instance, overstock.com charges a flat fee of $2.95 for most location in the United States regardless of what you bought.

What is table rate shipping?

This might appear a little complex, but I will walk you through it. Consider this example a retailer's point of fulfillment is somewhere around Birmingham might decide to charge client within that proximity a regular shipping fee of $5 on every order and the more the distance extends, the higher the shipping fee gets.

Live rates from a carrier

The live rates allow you to cover the cost of shipping and still offer your client the best rate they can get. With the use of the live rate from your carrier, you can gauge what the best price you can offer your customer is. It is way challenging to use this approach as a promotional offer considering that each client have different products and it can impede your judgment. The best method is to ensure you've been rational with your price and also looking at your surrounding and see the pricing setup of your competitors. This doesn't stop you from putting certain conditions into play such as the surcharge which covers for packaging and other extra charges incurred.

<u>Alternative shipping options</u>

Find the balance amidst all the options you have at your disposal will help you see ways you can offer promotional offers and still stay on top of your revenues. Consider the following alternative shipping opportunities:

- Standard + express (shipping)

- Free + standard + express (shipping)

- In-store pickup + standard shipping + same day delivery

- Freight + standard (shipping)

The challenge every successful e-commerce faces

There is no doubt that offering a free shipping option is one of the challenging aspects of e-commerce.

Let's take a look at the following statistics which is an excerpt from

188

Pitney Bowes 2015 Holiday season:

1.   95% of customers want a shipping option in their transaction option

2.   88% believes waiting on free shipping for 5-7 days is way better than 1-2 days of express service

3.   Between 3-5 customers have opted their purchase to qualify for a free shipping option

4.   68% admits to having used a free shipping coupon code.

Is free shipping a requirement for merchants?

This might appear a little tricky since making money is the focal point of every e-commerce platform. Then how would merchants achieve this without the endearment of shipping? I have dealt with quite a few clients who enjoy getting free shipping and still I was able to deal with the excess with my team members. And with our experience, we've been able to help over a thousand merchants curb their excesses when it comes to offering free shipping.

I will outline some necessary steps that can assist you in offering free shipping and making your money at the same time:

1.   Evaluate your market space

In most cases, you might not need free shipping to win customers over especially if you're running a b2b platform. All the customer wants in most cases is uniformity in pricing. When you have customers that are willing to stick with you, no free shipping offer will take them away.

189

2.   Does free shipping increases your market sales or not?

It is essential to analyze if free shipping is becoming an item of expenditure, cost of commodities or a combination of both. Is it creating conversion for your business or drawing up expenses?

3.   Make free shipping zonal based

Take a cue from jet.com they only offer free shipping to a specified location in the United States.

4.   Increase your express delivery

You can arouse the interest of the customer to the point of checking out where there will be a wait for 10days due to free shipping. Then increase the express delivery so that it balances the free shipping offer

5.   Make a monthly evaluation

Do your checks and balances on a monthly basis, going through the daily checklist might get you worked up after seeing your profit margin. But it's best if you make it a monthly affair, this will help you understand areas where you can work on.

6.   Display time of delivery

Everyone in the world can't stomach the thought of ordering a product and waiting over a week to get it delivered. So, when you display your delivery time for free shipping, it will spur your customers to settler for the fast delivery which you must have increased to a reasonable level.

7. Use terms and conditions

You can do this by setting a price tag on some specific product, and they're the only products that get free shipping. You can also make the low priced product on your site to get the free shipping.

8. Use different promotional offers

There are several ways to test out promotional offers but its good you figure out which sits out well with your market. You can upload table rates of your carrier and offer 20% shipping discount on the product. There are several offers you can combine until you figure which works out best for you.

9. Find a good shipping solution

Get a shipping solution that puts both your interest and your customer's interest into consideration. One shipping solution that readily comes to mind is shipperHQ. Your customers have assured an incredible customer experience.

Chapter 21:

Hiring a virtual assistant for your E-commerce Business

Introduction

The start of every enterprise requires putting in extra effort to meet up with your primary responsibilities which include meeting your client demands, managing your social media platform, and a host of other activities. It is possible for you to get swamped up with doing so much and unconsciously start paying more attention to work and less to yourself. This is one area where a virtual assistant comes in handy; an individual that assist in running your business and not necessarily developing it. See them as an extra help that shares the burden that comes meeting your business demands. Every entrepreneur, need support that will help you undertake specific responsibilities that comes with the smooth running of your enterprise.

Who is virtual assistance?

An individual that plays the functional role of managing a section of your business that is related to the online space. For business owners who don't have the financial strength to absorb an employee then a virtual assistant will always be a viable option. The apparent contrast between a VA and a full-time employee is the extensive research a virtual assistant does on a section of your enterprise. And the fact that, their charges are affordable and their services are top notch. It is natural entrepreneurs to get possessive with their business which is fine, but for you, to be productive, you need a VA to draw your attention and correct things you don't pay attention to.

What can a virtual assistant do for you?

The responsibility of a virtual assistant doesn't stop at the administrative wing of a business, and they can go as far as managing sales and social media platform for your business. Give your VA the needed guidance to enhance their effectiveness in giving an incredible service delivery. An intelligent VA can make something huge out of a minuscule amount of information.

The following are a few tasks you can deputize to a virtual assistant:

Social media management

Provide content across all platforms used by your business, read and respond to comments. Basically, everything that concerns your social media platform.

Customer care agent

Receiving calls and proffering solutions to the needs of customers.

Extensive research

Reach out to influencers that can help promote your business and searching for stats that you can use to spice up contents on your landing page.

Cold calling

Reaching out to prospective clients and getting their point of view about your product with the aid of scripted questions and answers. They set up a meeting between the potential clients and you.

From the tasks outlined above, you can see that the degree of relieving you're getting from the services of a virtual assistant is incredible. You will be saving more time that you can channel into something productive.

When is it appropriate for you to seek the services of a virtual assistant?

Hiring a virtual assistant is a tentative process, you must have had a first-hand experience of getting involved with your business. It will help you provide that detailed guidance to the virtual assistant you will be hiring. Figuring the proper time to hire a virtual assistant is as important as hiring one. Here are instances that might require you hiring a VA:

You realize that an extra hand will take your business to a whole new level.

You have cash set aside to employ the services of a virtual assistant.

There is a specific task such as the role of customer care which doesn't come naturally to particular individuals; such people can hire a VA to give their customers an impeccable service delivery.

You have your 9-5 job on the side, and your business is gradually making it mark, all of these summed up is draining the life out of you. The only viable option is to get a second hand.

You have the full knowledge of what your niche entails and explaining to someone how best to go about it won't be a problem for you.

You've taken out time to explore the nook and cranny of the featured apps on Shopify such as ifttt, zapier, kit and you realize that it's best to outsource this task.

Owning an e-commerce platform is a big task that takes time to actualize fully. For most businesses is a continuous exercise and it's vital you remain prolific as much as possible. Adding the function of customer service with this is a bit too much. Finding very means to keep your customers by always being at your best behavior, can drain your mental energy. Your best option is to hire someone that has the skillset to keep your customers satisfied.

Think of other areas where you can spend those productive hours you will spend listening to customers complaint and providing solutions. You can channel this into other aspects of your enterprise.

What should be my budget, if I plan on hiring a VA?

The amount you will spend on hiring a virtual assistant depends on the type of service you want. However, it is vital to note that oversees virtual assistant are less expensive in comparison with their Americans contemporaries. The American VA have a general pattern of payment depending on how you want the service. It can either be an hourly project basis and a flat rate option. Be informed that hourly is the most viable option especially when you're on a budget. It also helps you to monitor the output in correlation with the hourly cost. Another diligent approach is to find an international VA. They charge lesser, and you will be guaranteed an incredible working experience. When it comes to hourly cost, the prices could go as low as $3-$10 on an hourly basis. No doubt that is spending less for more value. Ensure you keenly examine the person you're hiring before making that move, see if they possess the skills you require from a virtual assistant.

One last option is hiring an "executive assistant," but this is solely meant for those who are extremely busy and require someone to do more than a VA will do. The executive assistant will take up several responsibilities in your business and take care of some personal errands you can't handle. Take your time to do research and ask questions before jumping on any platform to hire a virtual assistant. Whichever platform you're hiring from as so much to do with the extent you and your client would last.

Bringing a virtual assistant onboard

This is where the significant bulk of work lies for you because you're absorbing someone from different background and exposure that might necessarily not align with yours. The best approach is to document what you expect from the virtual assistant carefully. This should be backed up with a recording so that the VA would have a visual perception of what you have documented.

How to handle accurate documentation before outsourcing:

You will be assured of a minimal amount of errors when you carefully outline what is expected of the virtual assistant. But having it documented first will make it easier to write them out as a guide so that they can carefully follow through every step of the way.

Another way is using an on-screen recording to show each step they need to follow in achieving specific tasks, especially those that are repetitive. This will also help you to get inundated with the steps you will be communicating with the virtual assistant. Positions such as social media management, customer care representative that will require constant interaction with potential customers and clients. You will need to curate "predetermined responses" by searching for your past responses to clients, put them in shape and pass it along to your virtual assistant. It is best to give out tasks you can envisage it likely occurrence which will aid the mental alertness of your employee. You could document a scenario where "if this happens; then this should be your next line of action."

Platforms such as Facebook and Zendesk is a capable platform to find a virtual assistant, due to several success stories from entrepreneurs on how it has been beneficiary to the growth of their business. This implies that it is way more effective to use this approach than training someone from scratch.

The proprietary reason for hiring a virtual assistant is to bring relief, comfort to an entrepreneur and also have a sheer contribution to the growth of their businesses. If any of these things are absent, then you've not hired the right individual.

Making your job description attract the right type of virtual assistant

A good job description carefully outlines what you need in a virtual assistant; it's more like an amplifier and a magnet - attracting the right type of virtual assistant for your job. It makes your selection process seamless serving as your first point of filters. Here are some vital details that you should add to your description that makes it more directional:

-The degree of your enterprise

-Apps/tools they need to get entwined with

-Level of communication

-Experiences that will increase their success rate

-An outline of tasks they will perform

-Providing keywords that people search for regularly.

-Platform to hire a virtual assistant

Posting a job description for a virtual assistant on a general job offer page or forum might sound good but will not yield the required result since there is no measure of control on such page. Your best option is to visit a platform that it is specially designed for tasks such as this type. A platform that readily comes to mind is upwork; you can easily find the right kind of professionals for your job that is adequately equipped to handle your request. For those that are newbies in the hiring process, especially with Shopify store your best option is a platform that can help you find people who can pull off your project.

Using a platform like upwork gives you access to tools that can help you measure the output of your virtual assistant. The devices include:

Sellers review to check other customers experience based on their gig.

• Time tracking features to quantify their working hours in correlation with the amount paid

• Inbox and chat section to share files and discuss.

• An escrow service that ensures sellers only get paid once they've satisfactorily completed the job

- A stress-free mode of payment and invoicing.

As soon as you have completed the posting, extend an invitation to prospective virtual assistant pitch into your posting. When the messages start rolling in, then the vetting process can kick in fully. You should make an interview a requirement so that you can test out their communication skills and other things related to engaging clients on their page. If you feel the review appear vague and you need something more concrete, then reach out to their past clients to get firsthand experience of their client-customer relation.

The best way to manage a virtual assistance

After getting them up to speed with what is required of them, then you need to create a regular means of communication (slack, email, hangout), there as so many options to choose from. At this junction, ensure that you're giving them only what they need to perform their task effectively, access to social platform and e-commerce store is good enough for their work. Maintain a maximum level of security when dealing with your virtual assistant, don't grant them access to your financial account and lock down access to places you feel require top administrative access.

A popular platform like Shopify, facebook, and zendesk comes with features that can restrict the activity of a second party on your platform.

We will discuss practical steps one can limit access on individual platforms.

Shopify Store

When it comes to Shopify store, all that is required it to register your virtual assistant under a staff account and use the options to limit them to particular aspect of your store. Granting them access to only where they need to belong.

Facebook

Right on the facebook page manager, you can grant them limited access to where they will need to where they can post content to your facebook page.

Zendesk

On zendesk and more like other platforms, you will create an account for them as a new user where they can respond to customers queries, feedback, and complaint.

Another reality is that virtual assistant functions more like freelancers which imply their services are not exclusive to you alone. In light of this, it is advisable you compel to sign a non-disclosure form that keeps them from selling you out to your contemporaries. Upwork has this contained in its terms and condition section. You can revisit this part to be sure is part of the binding factor that holds you and your virtual assistant.

The significance of time tracking

The only viable means to ascertain the productivity of your VA is with the aid of a time tracking device. Although there are tools such as toggle with the time tracking features, it can't be as grandeur as what upwork has on their platform. This is in no way implying that you should always be at the neck of your VA, continuously monitoring their work schedule. But checking on them at intervals to see how well they're faring and areas where you can help to make their work better.

It gets to a point where your VA gets so used to your job like the back of their palm, that they begin to offer more productive suggestions that can help to grow your business. You will also get used to them that you will find it difficult to find a replacement, in case they have other things to do. Working with a prolific and intelligent VA will get you geared to either give them more responsibility or employ another VA.

Some other platforms to get virtual assistance

Upwork is fantastic, no doubt about that. But there are still other exciting platforms where you can get professional VAs. This might sound surreal to you, but some platforms house professional VAs just like upwork at an affordable price. For a quick personal errand or a one-time job, visit fancy hands; you will get first-hand assistance from VA experts. In most cases, your arrangement with the VA will be temporary since they get recycled often.

Another platform available only in the united states is Zirtual. You will get administrative virtual assistance that runs both your business and personal errand at a sum of $384 on a monthly basis.

There are so many more of this platforms that comes at a meager cost, but the only drawback is that you will have to search for time tracking and other tools that enhance productivity.

Inculcate the habit of delegating tasks

When you consider the amount of resource you had to expend in bringing your business to this stage of development, it is natural for you to feel possessive and never imbibe the culture of delegating tasks. But for you to enjoy a balanced life/work which is lacking in most entrepreneurs you need to learn to let go. You will not only be doing yourself more advantage, but your business will also experience a sporadic growth, which is the sole purpose of every enterprise. The moral of the story is to learn to delegate tasks.

Chapter 22:

Drive Traffic To Your E-Commerce Website Using SEO

Introduction

SEO stands as one essential tool that generates a high return for most online stores. However, most e-commerce has built their traffic generation tactics on social media and paid campaign. This method also works very fine, but it requires constant monitoring, and it takes a lot of money to put together. With search engines you go through less stress, all that is needed is some exerting some effort aforetime. I know it sounds concise and straight to the point, and you might probably be fantasizing about getting started already. I'm here to put you through what you need to know to have a beautiful Seo experience. Join me while I pilot you through it rudiments.

What is SEO?

Search engine optimization(Seo) can be regarded as the scientific process of getting your website optimized through the use of specific keywords to get ranked on google. Almost everyone is familiar with Seo but has failed to utilize this crafty approach of getting ranked on search engines. Google, for example, is trying to provide, users, the right

204

answer to their questions, ensuring that the answer is satisfactory. Here is how to achieve this:

Do extensive research on a content that provides solutions to a wide range of questions

You can use videos and images to provide a further understanding of your answers

Make your website responsive and offer a topnotch user experience that is intuitive and creative

Ensure your site finds its way into the lips of everyone

Means Of Generating Traffic On An E-Commerce Website

Make sure the contents are engaging with beautiful descriptions of your products and with high-resolution images. You should have reviews on your page so that buyers can quickly get drawn to your market.

Make your page less cluttered, making it easily accessible for anyone who wants to purchase your platform.

You should offer your customers the privilege to compare prices with other stores without leaving your page to make further research on the cost of the product. They might end up getting something convincing from your competitors.

If you're in the business of providing for the needs of others through your online store, then you will get to the top position. A typical Google search result will list out google ads first, then organic result follows, and in most cases, people mostly click on organic results. 95% of users will restrict their search to the first page which implies that your only option is to be on the first page of google search. The dynamics in your use of keyword plays a decisive role in determining, how you can place yourself on the first page.

Make Extensive Research On Keywords

This is the rudiments of setting up an e-commerce store. At this point there are two vital factors which will help me determine how well you're faring in this regard;

1.   If you're using a keyword that is difficult and you might never get to the first page.

2.   If you use a keyword that doesn't get a lot of traffic or something buyers check out.

None of the options mentioned above is a wrong representation of what a right keyword should look like. A good should keyword must have a good conversion rate and reasonable search volumes. Before going ahead with your decision, it is vital to consider "customers intent." To uncover this factors: client intent, keyword difficulty, and search volume, here are three essential ways that can help you achieve that, they are; Amazon, competitor research, SEO tools.

We will begin by considering e-commerce dynasty.

1.   Getting keyword from Amazon

Once you type in your base search keyword, there will be so many search results related to the base search keywords. This is the best tool that can be used to decipher the intent of a buyer. You can use google docs, but it becomes complicated when you have thousands of product to search. Your best option is the Amazon keyword tool which helps you to automatically curate all auto list result for a product that you searched for. For every keyword that you search for you will manually check which should make it to the list of your CSV file. It will be a bad decision to get all the keyword results loaded on our page, and we will still filter for search volume, keyword difficulty, and intent.

Let us get a better understanding of other means if getting keywords.

2. Get keywords using competitor research

Check for competitors who rank higher than you on google, and you can logically sniff through their pages for ideas on keywords. You can check on their category and product page to get an idea on how they use their keywords. Don't get your site loaded with keywords from your competitors because they rank higher doesn't imply they've used the right keyword or used keywords in the best way.

3. Get keywords using ahrefs

One proficient tool for getting keyword is ahrefs. It has other functions which attest for its versatility. It generates competitors research, backlinks and a host of other uses. We will dig deep into other options, later but let's get an understanding of it can be used for keyword research. Once you get signed up, you will be able to put the URL of your site, click on the "organize search tab" This will help you curate keywords that allows your page and other similar pages to get ranked.

How to ascertain if you're using the right keyword

Finding keyword difficulty, search volume, and buyer intent might appear tricky especially when you're not using ahrifs which helps you generate all of this automatically. You can try the google keyword planner, to get CPC(customers intent) and rough search volume. However it doesn't give you keyword difficulty, so your best option is to use the ahrefs. It will help you keep an organized result that will help you in tracing out your content. You can keep an organized house through the use of keywords matrix, which allows you to arrange your search result based on traffic, keyword difficulty, and CPC.

Structure Your E-Commerce Website

Your e-commerce can be compared to conventional sale outlet, and the same way you will clean up your store and keeping things in check is the same you would do for your online store. Three basic rules pan out when creating your e-commerce website, they are;

- Maintain simplicity and scalability

- Use keywords result to create URL and subdirectories

Examples of bad e-commerce website

Without a doubt, any site that doesn't apply the golden rule is a poorly developed e-commerce website. And such website might not get ranked, and they will make navigation difficult. Such a site will have up to four clicks before moving from one category to another.

Example of a good e-commerce website

In contrast to the website mentioned above, a good e-commerce website follows the three golden rule strictly and ensures that navigation on their platform is seamless. Your homepage should connect well with other pages most especially your category and product page. This will help your page ranked since they're getting authority from your homepage.

Strategies for on-page SEO

The idea behind on-page SEO is to ensure that your keyword is placed strategically to enhance your SEO rank, we will discuss three strategies that every e-commerce needs to apply for on-page SEO, they are;

- On-page SEO for category page

- On-page SEO for product page

- On-page SEO for blog content

For on-page SEO for category page

This is an essential aspect of your e-commerce website, imagine a potential buyer coming in contact with your category page. This means they've access to all your product page. Let us take a look at how you can optimize your page;

- Inserting your keywords in your URL

Adding your keywords in the title tag

- Insert your keywords in the body of the page

- Insert keywords in a text describing your image

- Insert keywords in the metadata

For on-page SEO for product page

You can repeat all the process outlined for the category page for the product page with just slight addition and deduction.

- You don't need a banner image since you have a product image

- Instead of 300 words, I will recommend going up to 1000 words

This is purely based on the fact that Google is purely a research tool which and most top pages on Google have contents going over 2000. You might wonder why I recommended 1000 words instead of 2000. Writing a product description of 2000 words can be daunting so keeping it at 1000 words is just beautiful and backing it up with product reviews is just perfect. If you're yet to pay attention to the incredible opportunity that comes with putting reviews gotten from clients on your product page, then you're living deep under a heavy rock.

Carrying out technical SEO audits of e-commerce platforms

The whole concept of SEO doesn't stop at the use of keywords, but the smart auditing your page for working link, mobile friendliness, speed, and everything that can make your e-commerce website to be optimized. All of these requirements are easy to meet up with, once you have the right tools at your disposal. What Google wants is to ensure that your customers have a fantastic user experience using your webpage. Here are some essential tools that have helped me over time in getting ranked on google, I might not be able to go more in-depth on the mechanism of each but you can find out about each, and they're quite helpful:

1. Google search engine
2. Google search console
3. Ahrefs
4. Beams us up
5. Copyscape
6. Barracuda penguin tool
7. Title tag pixel width checker

Local SEO for online store owners

This will be helpful if you won a physical store or you are looking for ways to get local traffic, then this section falls perfectly into your description. Here are features that can help local store owners in this regard:

- Google my business profile

- Gather local citation

- Get local links

1. Google my business profile

This is an approach in which local business gets featured on a local search result. You only need to drop details of your business on Google's database. Details such as the address of store, website, operation hours, reviews and any relevant information that will make clients reaching out to you.

2. Gather local citations

In a way to prove to google you're famous in your locality, you will be made to provide backlinks of a popular website such as local news, media, store, hotel and so on.

3. Build local ranking

The local ranking is a way of getting ranked within your local sphere, and you can do that by getting your links on favorite local news outlet, associations, chambers of commerce and so on.

Content marketing

This is my best approach to using keywords in getting ranked. But in a way I can say it's a thing of different strokes works for different folks, consider this statistics for instance:

- 45% of online retailers say blogging is their top strategy

- 70% prefers getting to know about an advert from an article

- 68% of consumers get satisfied with a product only after consumption

This is an indication of the primitive function of content marketing in SEO ranking.

There are millions of ways to get organic traffic, but there are few ways to get organic traffic your only option is to get acquainted with SEO. Every online retailer needs a profound understanding of its mechanism. Achieving a simple SEO can bring to you additional sales than envisaged and you don't have to break the bank to accomplish this, you can wrap things up in less than a year. Every part of this guide has been solely curated to give you an insight into how you can get ranked using SEO. I know it can be overwhelming to get things right at the first attempt but with constant practice, it becomes part of you.

Chapter 23:

How much do you need to start a business on Amazon?

Introduction

This list is for you out there who is interested in starting your FBA private business. The list is primarily to help you plan and make an informed decision. I was once in your shoes, so I know how it feels when you have nobody to put you through things such as this. The list is detailed and comprehensive enough, touching every facet that will help you to be successful on your journey as a retailer on Amazon.

Cost of production

The cost of production comes first because let us be candid without a product there is nothing to sell. This is the phase where you might have to spend a lot of money, although it depends on the type of product you're aiming at, in most cases production takes most of the running cost. I always emphasize the kind of product that will drive sales to your business, and you should always direct your attention to such products.

- Lightweight commodities (below 2lbs)

- Small in size – to cut down the cost of shipping

- Price range falls between $20 and $50

- Do your research and decide, if its wants vs need products

- Must be reproducible and distinctive among its peers

- Comes with an increased sales velocity on amazon but a reduced number of rating

Going by the condition outlined above, it will be of best interest to you if you have the price range of your product falls within the range of $0.10 to $10. I want to be precise; I will choose $3. The essence of this is to maintain a reasonable ROI which is primarily your reason for setting up your business. I will also advise your unit of production starts between 400-500 units, at least for a start. This will give you the privilege to do a "buy two get one free" giveaway at the launch of your product, and you will also get a good ranking from Amazon. This will also prevent you from running out of stock before ordering your next shipment, so either way, it's a win-win scenario.

Doing the math, you will have $3 x 400 units = $1200.

Shipping

The cost of shipping a commodity vary greatly, and in most cases, a wide range of circumstance comes in play. For instance the mode of shipment which could either by air or sea and the weight and size of the commodity. All those are potent factors in determining the cost of shipment. Base on my experience, if you work closely with the conditions mentioned above, my cost of shipment always fall within 60-80% of my product cost. The cost of production has covered for both the declared value of shipment and price of shipping. For the sake of precision, we will go with 70% for the percentage of shipping.

Doing the math, we have 70% of $1200 = $840

This price covers for the cost of shipping for all the units of products.

Market research tools

The market research is the basis for every business, and this should have been where you begin even before graduating to the point of manufacturing your commodity. But starting with the cost of production will put you in the right perspective about the cost of production and the type of product you will love to sell for a start. There are quite a lot of research tools that you could use out there, but coming from someone who has been in the e-commerce business for a while I will tell you some specifics. These research tools I've been helpful to me in staying ahead of my competitors.

At the moment, I use viral launch's product discovery tool because it makes my work more comfortable with it cut-edge features such as the estimating revenue, calculating profit and measuring sales velocity. These platforms have everything you need to keep your online store as productive as possible. Talk of selecting a product, calculating returns, making keyword research, and giving your product that breakout through the use of it many deal breakers such as the "giveaway" options. They have a bumper package that will help you get launched in the most mind-blowing way from their beginner's package and up till their pro version. Each of this cost $29 and 99$ respectively. But base on my experience I will recommend you to go for the standard package, it has every tool to help you upsell your inventories as a beginner. In my opinion, every newbie should consider starting with the standard package. You will find tools such as product discovery tools and the market intelligence tools quite helpful. It is an extension to your chrome and what it does is validating and giving excellent ideas on products by considering the velocity of sales, reviews and a host of other options.

P.S: the cost of the intermediate level as at the time of this write up is $59

Owning an Amazon seller account

There is no doubt this is the most important of any step in becoming a seller on Amazon. You have the option of an individual sellers account or a pro account whichever falls within your budget. But I would recommend you get a pro account which will allow you to have a product listing and accommodates more inventory. The pro account goes for $39.99 on a monthly basis, but that is not an issue for now. Go and get registered, and link up your bank details to the account. There is one certainty, Amazon will be more than willing to give you a refund when you're yet to make use of the account. I remember I didn't use my account for the first two months of opening, but there were deductions for both months. I reached out to their customer care agent, they filed my report and refunded the deducted amount. So don't get yourself bothered when you get the deduction and you're yet to use the space, you will get compensated just as I did.

The professional account costs $39.99

Digital branding

Adding a professional logo adds spice and differentiates you from your competitors and make you a corporate store right on Amazon. You can choose to do a DIY if you're capable of designing a stylish logo that looks professional. But if you don't have the luxury of time to do that, you can get on freelancing site such as fivver, and you could get this done as low as $5 depending on your bargaining power. However there has been an increase in the prices of services on that platform, but you can still find sellers who will give you a reasonable price at a reasonable price.

Never be convinced into thinking getting a logo is not essential, it can be compared to having a traditional store without a beautiful display that indicates you own the store. Since you're aware of the fact that your business is competitive, you should always look for ways to do things that make your store stands out. And having a professional logo is a way of standing out, you're telling your client that you will offer them an exclusive service that beats any customer experience they might have heard. It's a way of passing a subtle message of being on top of your game and staying ahead of your competitors. Get the best customized digital logo, that captures what your store stands for.

The price of a customized logo is $40

Universal product code

Every item needs a distinct universal product code, for it to be identified by Amazon. I will like to clarify a specific thing that keeps creating confusion among many with regards to whether you will be providing a unique code for every product. No, you're not providing a universal product code for the individual item that you have in your store instead it is a product for a listing. Lips have been jamming about Amazon not permitting the use of cheap barcodes and only recognize the use of GS-1 barcodes. This is a false statement. Amazon understands that some sellers on their platform are startups with small capital to run their business. The GS-1 barcodes cost around $250 which means which will increase your expenditure in getting capital for your business. I'm currently enjoying my cheap barcode which I use on my Amazon page, and it doesn't cost much. Getting a universal product code is not something you will have to break the bank over, with just $5 you will have your all your product tagged with a barcode.

Its okay to go with $5 for the barcode, some people say that they spend an extra $0.20 on the design of the product code on a single product. Under digital branding, I outlined some point that you find professionals in that niche to help you design everything that concerns branding which includes the barcode prints. Once you have the barcode, you send it to the designer, and they get it designed and printed out which you can paste on each product. The $40 you will be paying for digital design has covered for the barcode print. So all you will be spending on the universal product code is $5.

A total estimate of what you will be spending equals $2183.99, that's an approximation of $2200 to set up a professional amazon account. This amount is basic standards but doesn't nullify some alternative cost that could be incurred. This takes us to the final and last stage of starting up an Amazon account.

Alternate Cost

1.   Item photography

Have heard people slug it out when it comes to getting a professional photographer to snap your items for listing. I'm telling you this part is entirely optional and it depends on your choice. I take most of my pictures myself, and they always come out great, I will spend that money and use it for something else. If you're opened to do it yourself, then you will not find time to take an eye-popping image of each of your product. You can get professionals from places like fivver to help you handle things such as this. Ensure you get your supplier a sample of what is acceptable on Amazon before they begin work. The price sometimes varies between $15 - $100, it depends on how good you're with bargaining and the photographer you choose to settle for.

Since we're on a budget and we're just starting let us keep it at $100 for five photos.

2. Inspection charges

This doesn't bother you in no way if you type of product doesn't require getting inspected. Take, for example, suppliers selling small product might not need to get their product checked for any reason. If your supplier has a good record of good items without inferior goods, then you're good to go. Products that come easy and doesn't take time to manufacture doesn't need inspection as well. The products that will require inspection are the massive electronic set or goods that are susceptible to breakage will need to be duly checked before it is moved to amazon warehouse. This aspect might have been tagged optional, but it is vital to inspect the product it is being tagged for delivery carefully. Getting a product checked shouldn't cost more than $100 at most it will be $300 don't allow anyone to play a fast one on you.

An addition of $100 (for inspection charges) will be added to the initial sum of $2200 will make a total of $2300. That right there is what you need to set up a standard Amazon store.

All of these processes outlined are necessary steps and the respective amount needed for your Amazon account. Depending on your affordability rate and how much you are willing to invest, the total amount varies. But putting it on an average, you will be spending within the said amount. One thing is sure, putting all these procedures into use will generate a good ROI for your business. I'm a testimony to that, and I appreciate how my research helped me in making informed decisions. Do your research and begin to make substantial returns from Amazon.

Chapter 24:

How to sell more on your product page

Introduction

Most business pages have different kinds of pages such as the home page, about us pages, product page and so on. Some have the belief that the home page is the first page your readers encounter with your website. However, with the introduction of search engines, we've realized that any of your pages could be your clients first point of contact. Whenever a visitor is coming across your website for the first time, they accepted to see content that will enchant them, probably get attached to your product at the first point of contact. They are thrilled and willing to drop their details on your pages, all thanks to the engaging content you had sitting right there on your page. Hence, the rationale behind a client getting to your website through any page led to what we have known as "the landing page." We have got a host of ways through which traffic are generated to a landing page which includes organic search, social media post, emails and so on. More so, it is vital to emphasize that not all websites her landing pages, but we have those that are categorically designed to serves as the landing page where traffics gotten through paid search, or PPC campaign is directed.

PPC landing pages are essential purely because you're paying for every traffic that comes to the page, and every e-commerce store owners expect to get good traffic on their landing that measures up with that amount spent. In the light of this, we will talk about discuss e-commerce landing pages in correlation with conversion rate for PPC campaigns. The top guns of the e-commerce industry, even supported the theory that says each paid per search must have a unique landing page.

The Difference Between A SAAS Page And An E-Commerce Landing Page

A saas page is a dedicated landing page that is directed towards a single product. This page is easy to customize since it is primarily directed to the conversion of a single product compare to the paid per search campaign. The e-commerce landing page is somewhat tricky to handle since you're customizing landing pages for different products, in some cases it could amount to over 500 products. That is why you see a growing number of e-commerce websites using their product pages as landing pages.

A recent study shows that 61% of buyers directly search for products on their page instead of going through the hurdles of visiting an e-commerce website. The implication of this is that every product page must be cleverly written, so that the product title or description would appear on search engines.

Vital Things To Take Cognizance Of Before Starting A PPC Campaign

Taking a buyer down to the product page of a product, they would love to purchase, is an amazing approach to stacking up prospective buyers for your products. Some fundamental elements which you should pay attention to are the responsiveness of your page and providing detailed content. There might be a host of other rationales why buyers might withdraw their interest at the conversion stage, but keeping things clear and straightforward holds an advantage. There are cases where buyers lose interest, due to the complexity of your page, too much technical complication kills the interest of prospective customers. Another aspect is the skepticism that comes with dropping credit card details on your page. You've to ensure that your page doesn't give clients any cause for despair. You're halfway into winning buyers over once you check your boxes regarding the factors mentioned above. But there still lies the issue with shipping fee and time of delivery. If the cost of shipping sounds unbearable, then customers might leave your page and then, when the time of delivery seems it will take forever the customers might also withdraw their interest. If you've all of these handled, then we should dive straight into primary elements that make a product page function as an active landing page.

225

Six Fundamental Elements That Make A Productive Page Effective

- A dignifying product title that matches with searched keywords

The most visible part of your product page is your headline, and it's the first point of contact with your customer when they land on your page. It is vital that you make your product name distinctive(it should bear the name of your product) while still making it look just the way a prospective buyer will search for it. It is only a good headline that will drive the attention of buyers to your sales copy, once that is lacking then there will be no call to action.

- A detailed and well-structured product description

- Provide a detailed makeup of your product; sizes, shapes, material type and so on.

- Analyze the process of usage.

- Outline the advantage that your product can bring to your potential buyers.

A detailed description naturally buys the heart of the buyer which is one way you can hedge your competitors even if your price comes a little higher. What makes you stand out from other sellers? Why should they buy from you and not others? These questions will help you encapsulate the needs of your client in your product description. You can as well make use of your description in your PPC campaign, which will help you draw the attention of potential buyers to click your link.

- High-resolution popping product images

Your product image is a way to help your buyers have a feel of the authenticity of what you're bringing to them. Invite a professional to help you capture beautiful images that can attract the attention of buyers. Finding someone to use the product while you take convincing photos, using videos will make the buyer create a mental likeness for the product. A conventional store will always keep every part of the store neat and tidy to win the heart of customers. The same logic applies to online stores, having a good font and beautiful colorful scheme is not enough without enchanting images.

- Convincing shipping policy

A good shipping policy will always make buyers patronize you, especially when you back it up with fast delivery. However, this might not apply to all product, but you can place set a limit or make it a location-based offer. People don't have that much patience in the world, once they request for a product they want it delivered as quick as possible. Another aspect is indicating if there is limited stock of a product, this will create a mental impression that they need to get the product immediately not to lose out form the offer. When carrying out your PPC campaign, it is imperative that you make all of this visible.

- Make your payment policy unquestionable

Any trace of dishonesty in the payment policy of an e-commerce platform makes the client withdraw their interest. It is vital that you give your buyer an array of options, don't limit them to a payment policy that is not widely accepted. Third-party payment platform like PayPal has won the heart of many because it shields the data of buyers from an e-commerce platform.

- Reviews offer virtual proof

Customers want to know, how it feels like using your product before getting to the stage of purchase. The only way they can get this is through other buyers experience on the product through review. While this is coming last of the five options, it still stands as the most effective tool in a productive page. This makes it vital to add authentic reviews of your buyers on the product page whether positive or otherwise. Comments from social platforms can also help buyers to connect with their peers to get an understanding of how the product has been beneficial to them.

The process involved in connecting a PPC campaign with a product page

If you're planning on running an ad that connects a PPC campaign to individual product message, then you should follow the following steps carefully:

- Uniformity in your content

Pay close attention to your ad, making sure that there is a close connection between your ad and the information on your product page. When customers find their way to your product page, they will be relieved that they've indeed found what they wanted. In digital marketing, this is regarded as a message match. E-commerce sites whose PPC campaign doesn't correlate with their ad headline or product page are getting customers confused.

- Research on your keywords

With extensive research, you will have a good understanding of what buyers search for, and you should ensure your product campaign is filled with a lot of it. But getting the dynamics of this require checking out what clients search for and you can choose to be professional in the manner in which you use them. Check for relevant keywords and drop those that are seldom used. Using a different variation of this puts you in good light of having your product being searched for by a prospective client.

- Making your product category page into a landing page

No doubt product page is a valuable tool that brings sales to every e-commerce platform, but it has its shortcomings. The downside of this tool is the way it shades other product from making it to the limelight. This is also to the detriment of other sellers by depriving them of the opportunity of seeing other product that meets their needs, limiting their shopping options. This is where the function of the product category page comes in, one vital tool that have helped customers in meeting their needs. The category page captures a host of product which gives customers the liberty to choose whichever products they desire. And that offers better opportunities for conversion. Potential customers can compare products and see which meets their needs, so they can make an informed decision when about purchasing. Although this page is voided of social proof, there are star indicators which is an indication of the interest of buyers.

The best approach for connecting your PPC campaign with your product category page

Connecting an ad campaign to a group of products takes the same approach in connection to a single product. But in this case, you will limit the extensive use of keywords by using keywords that captures all the product that is displayed on the page. You can be as generic as possible, using words such as "leather baby shoes" is permissible for a product page. Avoid using a particular brand, and this will neglect the importance of a product category page and possibly take you back to a single product page. If there are special offers or discount that covers for all the product on display, then the product page is the best place to display that. Unique shipping options will also come in handy.

Take every page as a point of sale

Do you know every page on your e-commerce site could bring in good conversion to your sales? There are prevalent cases where you have prospective buyers check out a product on your page but prefers to purchase with their desktop computer. To curb instances such as this, your best bet is to create a call to action button on your product page like "add to wish list" this will create some commitment for the buyer instead of finding solace on another page. Remember we're in a fast-paced world that's why we have buyers coming to the internet for purchase, ensure your page fast and not overly loaded. You can create other sign-up options like the use of social media page like Facebook and Twitter or offer them the option of your signing up to your email list.

Some SAAS landing page write-up talks about the explicit restriction on your product landing page. This is in no way an advantage to an e-commerce store and could limit the option of potential customers from checking out other products. This implies that revamping other pages to have the feel of a landing page will be most advantageous for your e-commerce store.

Every option outlined above is vital for every e-commerce store in making right turn around in sales with the aid of their product page.

Chapter 25:

Tips for Facebook Ads

Introduction

Throughout a year, I got an intense knowledge about Facebook ads, particularly about how to make effective ads that brings a high conversion rate to your store. It was a rough journey, and I thought it was going to be a walk in the park. I made poor judgments which made me spend so much on certain ads. But in summary, it was a period where I learn so many tricks that helped sell so much that I could have imagined. With all this lessons and experiences gained I can categorically say, i have a broader understanding of Facebook ads. I prepared this write-up as a way to capture my experience while running Facebook ads and I will love to share ten of my biggest lessons with you.

1.   Run a worldwide campaign

Let's face the fact. There are so many countries that exist on the surface of the earth that we know nothing about their existence. Some countries can help you make a huge turn around in your sales, with a high purchasing power in comparison with other highly populated countries. The trend in e-commerce is leaning primarily on the big 4; Canada, Australia, United States, and united kingdom. These are the important countries most people limit their ads too due to their population. If you want to achieve bigger than you need to pay attention to the so-called underdogs. My first worldwide campaign, I took up the bold step of removing the big four from my market target making me streamline option only to the least foreign countries. But someone might have questioned my decision about navigating an online campaign from united states which presently has 325.7 millions of people. My primary reason was to ensure that the predominant countries don't distort other countries from accessing the account. Never make the mistake of running your ads primarily for the audience of the united states, Canada and the rest. You have your potential customers in any of the other international countries and less within the big 4.

2. Your funnel deserves more credit than you give

There are specific vital components that are essential in helping customers discover your products which in every way hedges facebook ad. The essential components include market funnels, prices of pitching your products to potential customers and the buying stage. All of the elements mentioned above are important than Facebook ads. The funnel is more like an end to a means and what it requires is putting all perspectives that will make your page attract buyers, once the Facebook ads bring them to your link. The product page is the best point of sale and should be prepared as a landing page. You can steer up the interest of a buyer by creating a bit of urgency with "offers while stock last" or a timer. I experimented this and wasn't sure at first what the outcome would be like, but it did contribute to the sales of our products. Learn new persuasive skills to make customers buy more products or go for an expensive product, with this you can increase your average order value. The performance of your Facebook ads is based on how well you've prepared your online store most importantly your product page.

3.   Make out time to work on your online store

My advice for you is to make out time to work on your online store and less on your facebook page. Let us be realistic, your product page is where the conversion happens, is the only place where buyers can visit to get a closer look and detailed information on what they're about expending their resources on. It is best if you put your page in the best shape possible. Think of the number of people who will have access to your product link, friends will share with friends, and the good message keeps spreading. And it would be disappointing when they get to your page and find things in complete disarray or not get as much information as they might have wanted. A Facebook ad is a single avenue and wouldn't record the success rate you will get from your product page. On a weekly basis, you should ask yourself, "what can I do to make my online store bring more sales?"

4.   Direct buyers straight to your product page

You might be wondering why i keep repeating product page so many times; it is your point of sale. And it is the first page on your store that should get optimized. Quiet often newbies in the e-commerce space find it challenging to differentiate a homepage from a product page. In most cases, this is what makes their page lack sales or bring buyers. You can never turn a click to conversion with a homepage, especially when the buyer is not interested in searching but have a specific product in my mind. Make sure you provide a link that is primarily directed to a particular product, to prevent your buyer from searching through tons of product. There are other benefits attached to this approach.

The first is that you can test the market-worthiness of a product. To see if it something people are geared towards buying. The final benefit is that buyers with a particular product in mind will be much pleased to get to your page instead of surfing through a wide pool of options.

5.   An engaging ad is vital for sales

There is no doubt it could be daunting when you have chunk load of likes and comments and zero conversion rate, I know how that feels. But having a lot of people in your comment section has its perks in a way. One of such is facebook taking notice of the engagement on your ad, and this creates the impression that people like your ad which makes Facebook cuts down the cost of your ads. There also lies the possibility of friends who tag their friends to have an interest in purchasing the product. Ensure you keep your comment section as engaging as possible. There is no rule stopping you from telling people to tag their friends.

6.   Keep things simple and classy

There are different forms of ads you can try out such as carousel, video or canvas ads. Each of these has pertinent roles they play in scaling your ad. But the most effective form of ads is the simple, classy style of ads. All you need is a high-resolution image of the product and a short, engaging message that calls potential buyers into action. My experience with Facebook ads thought me that keeping it simple works best all the time. It will be easy to direct your attention to a single product which is essential in getting a high conversion rate. Other options that we tested such as the video and carousel yielded few views, and in most cases, it readily appears as an ad. But a flat image with a short message easily blends with other posts on your facebook timeline. This is the primary reason why keeping facebook ads simple always work well over other forms of advertisements.

7.   Facebook is more of testing and less of optimizing

You can get a sense of what buyers are looking to buy with the help of facebook ad. You might not start to make much of a turnover in sales at the inception of the campaign. You might have to test out several products for you to make an informed decision on the which product to invest in. I tried several products, for a fact most of the ads I made were to test out what sort of product gets the attention of buyers. You should also try a different type of post, images, and products at intervals to ascertain what kind of approach is most appealing to buyers. Finding the right kind of product is not an indication that you should show complacency, there are other options of product that can still drive sales to your store but testing them out is the only way to get your facts checked.

8.   Scale your Facebook ads

Scaling you facebook ads depends on the success rate it had at inception. You might find it difficult doing this at first, I also had to reach out to mentors in that area to help with the scalability. Scaling an ad is different from increasing your ads budget. Take a close look at those ads that might be faring poorly, especially those with the lowest cost per conversion and low impression. Remove them from your original ads and create new ads that will be targeted specifically to that location or demography. Take for example if your ads make a low impression and low cost per conversion on Spain. Then you will create new ads, and the primary target would be Spain. But it is vital that you take out Spain from your original ads. When you inculcate this approach, it will be easier for you to scale your product without going through any technical rudiment.

9.   Scaling isn't a one size fit

There are some basic things to keep in mind when you're about deciding on a scaling an ad. Scaling is not implying that you will get a sporadic increase in your conversion rating, but it puts you in a good position. When you scale an ad with $10, and you were able to make ten sales, this doesn't imply that you will earn 20 sales with $20. In most cases, only scaling that comes with big budget feels the impact of the scaling. As I have mentioned above, you will need to put in little amounts to help you keep your conversion from going down abruptly. It might just be as little as $5 on a daily basis to keep your impression in check. It is vital to note that the more you spend on scaling, the more it becomes difficult to accomplish. You will find it very easy to double your $5 contribution to make $10, but it will be challenging to increase $500 into $1000. It is imperative that you take things slow and keenly consider the amount of money we've spent on conversion, which will shape our decisions.

10. Use separate pixel for individual product

For the newbies, you might want to sit this one out for now since it requires a measure of experience to get things right. Facebook pixel avails you the opportunity of creating a pixel of your customers based on their trading activity when in your store. You're building a pixel of your audience based on the data gotten from your store. This might not be effective for all business especially those who sell multiple products that involve that both genders use. I will advise you to make use of the pixelbay app on Shopify store which will help you build distinct pixel for your customers. Now consider this instance, if you own a store that sells both female and male clothing. It will be a poor business judgment when you use the same lookalike audience which will in most cases bear bad results. You can purchase custom made lookalike audience for your product page. This implies that you can have different lookalike audience for a single store directed to a different gender. Another approach is using the details of Facebook users who are visiting your site with the user through the link you used for your campaign.

Conclusion

The antidote in becoming successful with a Facebook ad is to continually try even if you didn't get a successful outcome. Once you're persistent with the ad, you will get better. Try every means possible either by experimenting different product, targeting options, captions, copy, and so on. I've tried most of this approach, and they've been adequate for my online store, it will also work for you just fine. Don't get reprehensive about trying new things and making mistakes. Every lesson in this book is my firsthand experience while trying to find my way around Facebook ads. It has been nothing but amazing.

Chapter 26:

How To Contact Instagram Influencers

Every Guru in the PR faculty who has had a great stance in the marketing world knows that the right way to establish and grow your brand is through pitching it to prospects, going through a formal press release and maintaining a follow up. Moving forward to 10 years later, I've noticed that the way branding works now is completely different from before. Well, I can only attribute this to the social media influencers as a whole, with Instagram Influencers as our case study.

Because of this new innovative trend, the fine line between public relations (PR) and marketing is either inexistent or very blurred. These days, Instagram is one of the biggest platforms on which you can use to endorse your brand. Hence getting a successful Instagram influencer to endorse your brand means you're already in the big leagues as your company has been established in today's grappling market. These social media influencers wield so much power and they can either make or break your entire company with just a post. Through this, you can be charged for a single post or even for a recommendation. However, advertisements worked differently in the last decade, you could only pay for it. But now you'll have to pay and hope the PR campaign does a good job with your target market.

Although social media has a very lasting impact on PR and marketing, this is why you need to tread carefully and analyze each move you're about to make. Nowadays almost everyone on the surface of the earth is a celebrity in their own little way because of the power of social media. But Instagram Influencers, in my opinion, wield the greatest power and have the largest impact on viewers. The public even looks up to them for their opinions before investing in any company or brand. They could even go the extra mile of boycotting particular brands because a certain Instagram influencer which they follow, has a different opinion about them. Well, you and I now live in a world where the sales of products can be reduced to nothing by these influencers, hence one needs to approach them with immense caution, the right attitude and in the right way.

Why should I contact Instagram Influencers?

First let's discuss this before we move on to *how* you can contact them.

Real fan base

If you want to reach out to celebrities in the course of marketing your product, you should know that these celebrities do not come cheap, hence you'll need a huge budget. Now, instead if breaking the bank for a celebrity to market your products, you can use these influencers who have an already impressive fan following. They are perfect for the job because they upload reviews about products and the best part is that they're human, just like you and I. In essence, these reviews that they dole out is the same thing as free publicity. Also, some of these influencers do not do paid promotions, they prefer giving honest opinions about certain products based on their personal preferences.

Products promotion to actual target audience

If you're like me then you should be asking 'what exactly can they do for me' by now. Having the support of an Instagram influencer can really be beneficial for both parties involved. Once your relationship with them is secure and valuable, they will help you by promoting your brand on their page and within their community. Some may even go ahead to promote it outside their community too. Also, if your brand or product is spectacular or if the influencer is passionate about it, they will not hesitate to defend it if the need arises.

In essence, whatever you're selling or rendering, make sure they really enjoy it. Here's the part that may bum you out, you cannot directly ask an influencer to endorse your product. This is because some of them do not actually do paid promotions, hence they get rattled once that is insinuated. This is what you'll need to do. You will need to orchestrate a scenario that will nudge the influencer into endorsing your brand by themselves. Also, ensure that the deal is one in which both parties are benefiting from. A scenario in which the influencer feels he/she is not receiving benefits equivalent to his/her loyalty, this influencer will likely stop promoting your brand and you'll have to look somewhere else for another influencer. Finally, your relationship with your influencer must be kept as professional as possible

A platform with great traffic

People are known to spend lots of valuable time on social media. It has indeed been proven that social media is the easiest way to get across to your target audience. Also, you should know this if you're considering paying for ads on Facebook or other apps. The truth is that most consumers are very skeptical about choosing a brand or using a product just because they saw an ad about it on Facebook. You'll need to come down to the people they know and can relate to, the influencer. People trust them 90% of the time. Even when they casually mention a product or recommend it based on it's capacity. An example of this is the beautiful and famous Kylie Jenner coming in her Instagram page to announce 'in love with my new fashionnova jeans' as a caption on her photo, rather than appearing on a TV commercial and saying 'because you're an icon.' You can see there's a crystal clear difference between both methods of advertisement. Being a potential buyer, you may ask yourself 'does Kylie really rock these jeans?' However if she casually mentions that she loves the new Jean line, you may likely think: If Kylie loves it, it must be of high quality. And this my friends is how Instagram can mold and change opinions.

Getting your brand endorsed on Instagram : The right way

The following are ways on getting your brand endorsed on Instagram by influencers. These eight ways are sure to get you the endorsement you deserve.

Put in the work and do some research

Some people may call this stalking, not I. You'll need to know what you're investing in. Not all of these influencers are polite or respectful, some are really rude and mean. Also, not all of them will enjoy this product you want them to endorse, hence you'll need to do some valuable research before you approach them. Let's start with your target audience, take a good look at your current clients and see if they fit the portfolio of your desired clients. Next, head over to their social media platforms and check to see the kind of influencers they follow. You'll also need to check the tweets they're retweeting, the pages they're liking and what they're actually talking about in their accounts. Once you've done this, go over to these influencers profiles and check them out. Check out their following and assess their posts. Based on your findings you'll need to answer some questions. 'Do you think this influencer is the best fit for your brand?' 'would he/she even like your product?' You'll need to figure this out.

Narrow your choices

It is actually smart to start with a large number of influencers you're interested in. Next, narrow it down to the ones who will be a vital asset in promoting your brand. I would suggest that you start with about 20 influencers first, then research about them accordingly. Also, Instagram is not the only social media platform, diversify into other platforms. Check for these influencer's blogs, Twitter following, Facebook fan base, also check if they have been invited by other parties to give their opinions. Kick it up a notch and check if they have recently been featured in any authentic, niche related magazine. This only gives the influencer greater credibility and make them worth an investment.

If you're into beauty or familiar with the beauty community as I am, you should know about Huda Beauty's Huda Kattan. She is really huge on Instagram. She is a blogger/ reviewer on the platform and people believe her every word. This is because she has built an empire from her name, she has a blog, speaks at different platforms and gets interviewed. Hence, people naturally go along with her recommendations and preferences. What I'm saying is that it is ideal if you know details about your potential influencer. Knowing them better will only give you ammunition to pitch your brand better to them. Lastly, ensure that they update content often and keep their followers engaged.

Email them

This is traditional but it is easy and it works too. If you want to contact your potential influencer, simply send them an email to their provided email address. Draft your email in a professional way explaining in details about yourself, your brand, what you aim for and your vision. Mention some reasons why they'll love your product or why they'll need your product in life. This is a professional email after all and you'll need to be as straightforward as you possibly can in the proposal. Make sure your proposal doesn't come off as a demand. Remember that you are asking for a favor and you still want their endorsement.

For this I'd suggest you leave the hot shots alone and go for those with a decent following but aren't huge celebrities yet. These ones are perfect because they still have an impact on people even though they're not totally there yet. You'll need to be prepared to receive a price list because not all influencers work for free. Hence, if you think a particular influencer is crucial in taking your brand to the next level, then you should consider paying for their endorsement, otherwise look for another alternative as they are limitless.

Mention them

Incase you were unaware about this, there are actual professional Instagram Influencers who make money off promoting brands. They even get paid to go on all expense paid trips just so they can go to certain places to endorse certain products/places and then return. If that is not budget friendly for you, you can stick with tagging their handles in your images or mention them in the comments. Their following is insane and so are their charges. So I will recommend that you mention them whenever you make a related post about your brand or even on something they posted. Go ahead to retweet their tweets and mention them on these social media platforms just to establish a good relationship with them.

Extend an invitation to them

Lots of these Instagram influencers actually love addressing crowds. They love being guest speakers and even the crowd loves listening to them. It is amazing to have content on their blog but remember that once you invite others to your platform, they come in with their followers. You can do this through a simple email asking them to grace your page as a guest speaker. This will give them a sense of belonging and accomplishment and you will also get lots of people talking about your brand with no financial cost to you. Remember, flattery can go a long way. Pick the right topic, sentences, even pictures to convince this influencer to key into your brand. The email you're sending should highlight your passion for your brand as well as how you feel about the influencer's honest opinion concerning it. I believe that out of all the influencers you end up contacting for this purpose, about half will appreciate you reaching out to them personally, as well as giving them a chance at honesty.

Create an interview

Creating an interview with your potential influencer will actually reduce their workload and make it easier for them to talk about your product. Because they love talking about themselves, this shouldn't be a problem. There's no need for him/her to draft a brand review for you, they can simply tell you over the phone while you write it down. We all know they're very busy people, hence you can put it together for them and they can talk about it when they're ready.

Instagram takeover

This strategy has been popular over the last year. It is when people ask Instagram Influencers to take over their brand's Instagram page. Here they get to talk about their experience with using the product and also drop reviews and pros. Although through this, the influencer brings a truck load of followers that will build your brand image, but you'll also need to be careful as this can be tricky on both sides. You'll need to plan carefully and the influencer also needs to be totally aware of your products and brand. Set this takeover in advance. You can also tease your audience by leaving little clues of who might be the surprise guest. Check all the boxes and nothing should be left till the last minute.

Send samples

This is the best way to reach out to an influencer. Pack your products as a gift, followed by a hand written note about your company. This will let them know that you think their opinion is important. Also, give them a proper background of your company, mention all your social media handles and product details. Your package should be very presentable because the aim is for them to feel a sense of connection with your brand, just so that they are drawn to try it out. You might be lucky and they love your product enough mention it to their followers.

Made in the USA
Las Vegas, NV
07 May 2022

48547890R00146